Searching for a Friend

by

Maria Quirk Walsh

Attic Press
DUBLIN

First published in Ireland in 1993 by
Attic Press
4 Upper Mount Street
Dublin 2

British Library Cataloguing in Publication Data
Walsh, Maria Quirk
Searching for a Friend
I. Title
823.914 [J]

ISBN 1-85594-088-4

Cover Design: Angela Clarke
Origination: Verbatim Typesetting and Design
Printing: Guernsey Press

This book is published with the assistance of The Arts Council/An Chomhairle Ealaíon.

Dedication

For my children Lavinia and
Thomas with love

About the Author

Maria Quirk Walsh began writing in 1988, after winning a Dublin Millenium short story competition. She has had several stories published in magazines and won the *U Magazine*/Irish Mist short story competition in 1993. *Searching for a Friend* is her first full length work of fiction. She lives in Dublin and has one son and one daughter

Prologue

Christina tossed and turned, unable to sleep. She knew now she could never trust them again, that it would always be the same. They'd pretend to be friends for a while, then just as she was beginning to think everything was all right, they'd plan some other spiteful trick. She should have told her mother from the very beginning, she realised that now. It would have been easier then, but now it was impossible. Her mother's work posed enough problems for her at the moment and she'd seemed particularly sad last night when she mentioned Dad's name during dinner. And Siobhán and Helen were such angels in their teachers' presence, she thought ruefully, never showing the mean, bullying side of their personalities. It would prove difficult to convince anyone of what they'd done...

Lying there, thinking of what had happened earlier in the day, she found it hard to believe that only a few months ago her life had been so happy and uncomplicated. Even when Áine had dropped her bombshell, Christina had never imagined that things could change so much.

Burying her head in the pillow, she tried to shut out all that had happened since then but against her will, her thoughts took her back...

Chapter One

'I just knew you'd do it, Christina. I just knew it,' Áine O'Neill said triumphantly as they made their way back along the crowded corridor to their classroom.

'I still can't believe it,' Christina replied, her voice filled with excitement.

They were returning from the school assembly hall, where, only moments earlier, along with all the other second years, they'd waited impatiently for Mr Doyle, the headmaster, to make his announcement. For once, the young people before him were interested in what he was about to say and shifted restlessly as he adjusted his spectacles and looked closely yet again at the sheet of paper in his hand before finally calling out the name of the winner, Christina Miles. A ripple of applause filled the hall, and dozens of faces turned in Christina's direction. Even though she'd heard her name being called out, for a second or two it didn't register with her that she'd actually won. It was only when people began to clap her on the back and congratulate her that the good news really began to sink in. After all the weeks of hard work and research, she'd come first with her seashore project.

'I just knew you'd do it!' Áine repeated for the third time, taking a closer look at the lovely pen-and-pencil set in Christina's hands.

'Hmm…A.T. Cross. Nice to see Mr Doyle practising what he preaches and presenting something Irish-made, and top quality too,' she said.

'Yes, it's really beautiful, isn't it, Áine? I'm glad you were here for this. It wouldn't have been the same if you'd been gone.'

'Yes, only another week together,' Áine reminded her, suddenly subdued at the thought.

Áine, at fourteen, was six months older than Christina. Apart from the fact that they both had blue eyes, and stood five feet two inches in their stockinged feet, they were as different as two girls could be. Christina was large-eyed with wavy dark hair to her shoulders. She was a good listener and the quieter of the two, while Áine was a red-haired chatterbox, always full of life. Despite their different personalities, they were the best of friends and had been since their first days together in junior school.

When school broke up at the end of first year, neither of them had any clue about the huge change that was to come about in Áine's life. The long summer days stretched invitingly before them and even Mr Doyle's announcement of a special summer project competition hadn't cost them a thought as they knew that it was up to each individual student whether she took part in it or not.

'You might just be glad of something to do,' he said at assembly the day before the holidays started, 'and there'll be a nice prize for the winner.'

Most of the girls had rolled their eyes to heaven at the thought of any kind of research or study during the weeks ahead. But as the days went by and the weather wasn't always as good as they'd anticipated, quite a number of them, including Áine and Christina, had begun to have second thoughts about taking part. Christina decided to start a project about the seashore.

One day, more than half-way through the holidays, when the two of them were on their way home from the library where they'd just spent most of the morning poring over anything they could find to do with marine life, Áine first told Christina she would be going away. Christina stared at her in disbelief.

'You're not serious, Áine,' she gasped. 'Come on now—stop fooling.'

But the look on her friend's face soon convinced her that what Áine was saying was true.

'Dad's lost his job. He's been expecting the bad news for a while, but he and Mammy kept it to themselves until they had to tell us...' She broke off, a slight tremor coming into her voice. 'Anyway,' she went on, taking a deep breath, 'we're going to live on my grandparents' farm. There'll be plenty of work for him there.'

'Lost his job? Gosh, that's really awful, Áine. But couldn't he try to get another job here in Dublin?' Christina asked, still unable to take it all in.

'He's been trying all right, but so far nothing's come up. With so many people out of work right now the chances of getting another job are pretty slim,' Áine replied dismally. 'And he hates farming, you know,' she went on. 'He always did. That was why he left home when he was a young man and came to Dublin. He thought he'd never get away from it and now he's being forced to go back. Anyway, Dad says we're not going to burn our boats. He and Mammy have decided they're not selling the

13

house straight away. It's going to be rented for a while until they see how things go. He's already put his name down with quite a few employment agencies and if anything comes up they'll let him know.'

Christina stood there silently as her friend continued talking. Áine's grandparents were looking forward to the family coming, she told her—she knew that from their letters. At least they had no worries that they wouldn't be welcome. The older couple were getting on in years and could do with some help in running their farm.

'They were just thinking about taking on an extra man when Dad got the bad news, but they've made it quite clear to him that if anything comes up in the way of a job, there's no need for Dad to feel he has to stay on and we can all come back to Dublin any time we like.'

'Well, that's something, anyway.' Christina didn't know what else to say.

'But I hate the thought of going, Chris, of leaving Glenwood and everyone, and I love it at St Mary's. But at least I'll be starting back for a week or so at the beginning of second year. When Mammy spoke to Mr Doyle, he said I should come into school right up until the day we leave. "The child would be far better off with the rest of her friends than moping about at home," Áine mimicked their headmaster's voice. 'Remember when our parents were deciding on which secondary school they'd send us to?' she suddenly asked.

'Will I ever forget?' Christina groaned. 'It was a nightmare. I was terrified we'd end up going to two different places.'

'And now here we are, being split up anyway,' said Áine bleakly, 'and there's not a thing we can do about it.'

'Are you sure there's no chance of a change of plan, that in the end you might not have to go?'

'Afraid not—Westport it is,' Áine said, her voice a little husky.

'Westport? You mean Westport as in County Mayo?' exclaimed Christina, up to now not having thought to ask exactly what part of the country Áine was going to. 'But that's miles away!'

'Well…a bit beyond Westport, as a matter of fact,' Áine admitted, biting her lip. And then, trying to summon a little of her usual bubbly good humour, in an effort to cheer them both, she added, 'Anyway, we won't be going for ages, not for at least six weeks yet.'

Six weeks had seemed like a long time then, but the days had flown and now, as they stood side by side in the school corridor, the excitement of Christina's win faded for the moment into the background, as they sadly had to face the fact that there was now only one week left.

'What time are you heading off tomorrow?' Christina asked as she sat curled up on Áine's bed.

'Some time mid-afternoon, according to Dad,' said Áine. 'Gosh, I never knew I'd accumulated so much stuff,' she muttered, as she tried to squeeze yet another bottle of Satsuma Bubbles from the Body Shop into her already overflowing washbag. 'Just as well Dad took most of our "effects", as Mrs Kenny would say, down with him last weekend.'

Christina giggled. Mrs Kenny was their year head at St Mary's and 'your effects' was one of her favourite expressions. Whenever the girls were changing classes she never failed to remind them not to leave anything behind and to be sure to take their effects with them.

'Sometimes I think she must say it in her sleep,' Áine said, flopping down on to the bed beside Christina. 'Still, she's nice. I hope my new year head over in St Columcille's will be OK.'

'St Columcille's. Is that what it's called?' For Christina it was strange to think that in a week or two Áine would be at a different school well over one hundred and fifty miles away. She looked around the comfortable, although somewhat untidy bedroom, and sighed. All the afternoons they'd spent here, sometimes studying, sometimes talking about pop stars or clothes, or just messing about with each other's hair. There were times when they'd had to jam a chair against the door to keep the twins out. Not that they'd got anything against either of them, but Karen in particular was always dying to know what Áine and Christina were talking about. And then there was that day Áine's mother allowed them to paint the walls whatever colour Áine chose. The primrose yellow had faded a little since then, Christina noticed, looking round her, but the few flecks of paint which they'd splashed on to the carpet and hadn't noticed until they were dry and almost impossible to remove, were still just visible beside the wardrobe.

She'd always thought it was only older people

who had memories, but now she realised that you didn't have to be old or middle-aged to have things to look back on. This room held enough memories to last her a very long time.

'I'll write every week,' Áine promised the following afternoon as she leaned out of the car window. Christina nodded, not trusting herself to speak, a huge lump in her throat now that it was actually time to say goodbye.

'Tell your mother we're sorry to have missed her, love,' Áine's mother said as the car started up.

'See you, Christina,' her younger sister Karen shouted, and as the car drew away Áine's father blew the horn furiously several times. Christina could see Thomas, Karen's twin brother, giving her a 'thumbs up' sign out the back window. Christina knew she was going to miss the pair of them a lot, too.

She stood at the front gate, waving until the car turned the corner and was out of sight. She didn't feel like going back into the house just yet. Somehow Christina felt that as soon as she did, and the hall door closed behind her, she'd finally have to accept the fact that Áine had really gone. So instead she wandered around the front garden, looking at the last few flowers still struggling to stay alive now that summer was over and autumn had arrived. An empty crisp bag that someone had carelessly thrown away blew across the lawn. She picked it up and finding nothing more to occupy her in the garden, crumpled it up in her hand and went into the house.

It seemed even quieter than usual to Christina as she stepped inside. Glancing at the clock in the hall, she saw it was just past four o'clock. Two more hours until her mother was home. Christina sighed as she made her way towards the kitchen for a can of Coke. She really wished her mother didn't have to go to work. There were times, too, when she dearly wished she had a brother or sister and, she told herself, as she took a sip from the Coke can, today was one of those days.

Christina's father, John Miles, had died when she was ten. He'd been an outgoing, fun-loving man, but gentle too. Christina couldn't ever remember him raising his voice. She'd thought the world of him and she could still remember the way he managed to keep his face serious even when telling her the funniest of jokes, although the glint in his light-blue eyes always betrayed his merriment. Because he died so young, his pension hadn't amounted to much and for the first couple of years after his death her mother, Angela, had struggled to make ends meet by running a small playschool. But about a year ago, she found herself with no choice but to go back to work.

'We need the extra money,' she explained to Christina. 'What with you going into secondary school, there'll be books and extras to be paid for and your uniform to buy. With all the bills we already have coming in, and the mortgage rates going up again, too, I've got to start bringing in more money. The playschool's not enough just now.'

But deciding to go back to work and actually doing it were two completely different things, as Angela Miles quickly found out.

'I hadn't a clue what to do,' her mother told her

18

after her first interview. 'I didn't know how to send a Fax, and when they asked me about word processing I thought I'd die of embarrassment. Those machines were only coming into offices when I gave up my job to have you,' she said, dismay written all over her face. 'There's no point in going for any more interviews, I'd only be wasting my time and the employer's time.'

After that her mother had decided to enquire about a place on a FÁS course.

'Better try to acquire a few up-to-date skills,' she'd said, making a face.

'Sounds like it was designed just for you, Mum,' Christina remarked, when details of the Return-to-Work course arrived in the post. 'Listen, it says here that the aim of the course is "To help mature persons who have not been in paid employment for some time to readjust to the world of work".'

'Here, let me see that,' her mother said, taking the piece of paper from her hand. 'Hmm, you're right. And I see it covers an introduction to computers. Now that would be very useful. And there's a session on interview techniques. I could certainly do with knowing a bit more about that,' she finished with a laugh.

Christina's mother had been lucky enough to secure a place on a course much sooner than she'd expected. 'Fourteen weeks! Well, I should certainly learn something in that length of time,' she commented to Christina.

Just before she completed the course, Christina's mother bumped into an old workmate while walking down Grafton Street on a Saturday afternoon. They chatted for a while and Angela learnt that there was a job going in the other woman's office, a large advertising agency. They wanted a mature woman and not a school-leaver. Things happened pretty quickly after that and within a couple of weeks Angela was back working full-time. Knowing that her mother had had no other choice, Christina smiled and pretended it didn't matter.

But it did.

Upstairs in her bedroom, Christina changed out of her school uniform and hung it carefully in the wardrobe, the louvered door creaking slightly as she closed it. Then turning to her bed, which she'd left unmade after rushing out to school at the last minute that morning, she smoothed the sheet, plumped up the pillows and pulled up the duvet cover. An old worn panda lay on the spare bed in her room and, reaching over she propped him up comfortably against the pillow. That was where Áine slept when she stayed over and she always joked that she only came so she could 'cuddle up to panda.' How long would it be before she'd be staying over again, Christina wondered dejectedly. Probably not for months, until they both had a long enough break from school. Looking over at the panda's almost threadbare face, she even imagined that he, too, looked sad at the prospect. And afternoons she and Áine had spent together doing their homework— they were all over now, too.

She flopped down on the bed and looked up at the Bon Jovi poster on the wall. There was an identical one hanging in Áine's bedroom, or had been, she thought ruefully, remembering that she'd seen her take it down the other day and roll it up carefully for its journey to Westport. They'd each bought one on 'The Night', as they always referred to it. What a night it had been! The date would be imprinted forever on her memory. Friday 21 May, 1993, the night Bon Jovi had come to the Point Depot. And she and Áine had been there, although it had taken quite a bit of persuading to get their parents to agree to let them go. A smile crossed Christina's face as she remembered the bruises she'd had on her arm the next day where Áine had squeezed it unknowingly as she listened in sheer ecstasy to Bon Jovi sing 'Born to be my baby.' Áine had stayed over that night and they'd talked into the early hours of the morning, reliving every moment of Bon Jovi's never-to-be-forgotten performance!

Christina knew she should get her books out and begin her homework, but for the moment she just lay there and continued to stare vacantly at the huge poster.

Chapter Two

St Mary's Secondary School was a walk of about ten minutes from Christina's house. It was a bright, modern, two-storey building, and was set quite a bit back from the road at the top of a tree-lined driveway. From the first floor, the pupils could see the red rooftops of Glenwood housing estate where most of them lived.

Christina's first day in school after Áine left for Westport turned out much better than she'd expected. As she walked into the PE hall some girls in her class called her over to join them. She hurried across to where they stood beneath the basketball post. They were in the process of choosing who should be on which team for a game. She knew all of them, but some of them not particularly well. She chatted to them occasionally, of course, but it had usually been Áine who'd joined in first and, as her best friend, Christina had automatically been included. But it was flattering to be invited into the group just for herself, and it was exactly what she needed that particular day.

'So Áine's gone then,' commented one of the group, a tall, thin, fair girl called Helen. 'Bet you'll miss her.'

'Yes, I'm sure I...' Christina began, but was interrupted by another girl whose name was Siobhán. She was attractive, olive-skinned, with dark bobbed hair.

'We always called you two the "Siamese Twins",' she said cheekily, her dark eyes flashing as she spoke, 'because where one of you went, the other went.

Always stuck together, get it?' Her laugh was shrill and Christina found it strangely out of keeping with her attractive appearance.

'I get it,' she replied with a slight smile, not sure if she liked the comparison.

'Come on, you three, stop yakking,' another of their group called across to them. 'We need three more on this team. Better take your places quickly or we'll get somebody else.'

It was two weeks before Áine's first letter arrived. Christina had been watching the postman for days, but each time she rushed to see what he'd put in through the letterbox she found it was just a bill of some sort, or a circular. But finally it did arrive and, picking it up quickly from the hall floor, she tore it open.

Dear Christina
I know I promised to write every week, but last week was so busy here, with settling in and everything, that I just didn't get a chance.

The farm is much bigger than I remembered it, and Daddy has more than enough work to keep him busy. We've all had to do the odd job or two, and I suspect we'll get more of that type of thing as we get to know what needs to be done around the place. But at the moment I think that with the way Karen, Thomas and I are handling the jobs we're being given, we're more of a hindrance than a help!

The farm is about four miles outside Westport in a little spot called Castledonagh. The McDonagh clan lived here hundreds of years ago and, yes, you've guessed it—there's an old ruin. You can see it from my bedroom window. We haven't had time to explore it properly yet but when we do I'll write and fill you in on all the details about it. See, I haven't forgotten that history is one of your favourite subjects.

I'm starting at St Columcille's on Monday. I went over with Mammy to meet the headmistress last week and to have a look around. It's not half as modern as St Mary's, but then it's been built for years and years. It was run by the nuns at one time, but there are only two of them still teaching there now; one teaches Religion and the other Home Economics. I'm hoping that Gráinne, who lives on the farm next to ours, will be in my class. She's the same age as I am. I met her in the village during the week and she seems quite friendly. I'm sorry this is such a short letter. There's lots more I could write, but Mammy is calling us for dinner just now, so it'll have to keep until next time.

Write soon and give me all your news and fill me in, too, on everything that's going on at St Mary's.

Love Áine

Christina read the letter twice before grabbing her schoolbag and, mindful of her mother's daily reminder before she rushed off to work, double-checked to see that she'd unplugged the electric kettle and the toaster, before giving the hall door a good bang to make sure it was properly closed behind her. It was great to hear from Áine at last, she thought as she walked along. She sounded happy enough from her letter. Christina was glad she'd met someone she liked.

She thought of Helen and Siobhán and of how lonely she'd have been these past two weeks but for their company. The thing she'd dreaded most when Áine had told her she was moving to Westport had been the thought of having no particular friend at school. To be honest, she'd been surprised at the speed with which Siobhán and Helen had befriended her, but greatly relieved not to find herself with no one at all.

Just then Christina saw the two of them a little farther up the road and began running to catch up.

'Hi,' she said breathlessly as she reached them.

'Oh, hi,' they greeted her.

Siobhán asked, 'What were you running for?'

'I just wanted to catch up with you two so we could walk the rest of the way together.'

'That's OK. For a terrible moment I thought you might be one of those swots. You know the type, never a minute late for school, can't bear to miss a second.'

'Any news from the other half of the Siamese Twins?' Helen cut in before Christina had a chance to think too much about Siobhán's sarcastic remark.

'Well, yes. As a matter of fact I got a letter from Áine just before I left the house,' Christina told them as they stood at the edge of the path waiting for a car to pass before crossing the road.

'Well?' the other two said together.

'Well what?' asked Christina, puzzled.

'How is she getting on, of course,' Siobhán snapped.

Taken aback by the sharp reply, Christina found herself stumbling over her words as she filled them in on what Áine had written.

Christina waited until the rest of the class had gone out into the yard before approaching Mrs Kenny. The year head looked quite nice today, she thought, as she made her way towards her through the desks when the last girl had left the room. When she wore her light brown hair loose, she looked much younger. Sometimes she wore it caught up in what her mother had told her was known as a French pleat. She and Áine used to spend ages some afternoons up in Áine's bedroom trying to guess how old she was, but all they really knew about her was that she came from Wexford, was a widow and had a daughter living in America. 'The Sunny South East' was another one of her favourite expressions.

'Yes, that's all right, Christina,' Mrs Kenny said in reply to her request. 'You can move your books after break.'

Christina thanked her and headed out into the school yard to join the others. She looked around, standing on tiptoe to see her friends. Although she couldn't see Siobhán, she could hear her name being called, just audible above all the other chatter that was going on around her. Eventually, after peering for several seconds in the direction from which the sound appeared to be coming, she spotted Siobhán, arms waving, calling her over.

'Well? Did she say it was OK?' she asked, when Christina had finally managed to fight her way through the noisy mass.

'Yes, she did. I can change seats from where I'm sitting and move over beside you both as soon as we go back inside.'

'That's great. Come on, then, we're in the middle

29

of an argument as to whether Miss Furlong's hair is natural blonde or dyed to bits,' Siobhán said, taking Christina by the arm and pulling her over to where Helen and a group of laughing girls were waiting.

Christina's mother, smiling at her daughter across the table that evening, said, 'Well, that was very thoughtful of Helen and Siobhán, I must say.'

'Yes, I'd never have dreamed of asking. I wouldn't really have had the nerve, but when Helen suggested that I should…well, I just did,' Christina said with a laugh, as she finally managed to wind an elusive strand of spaghetti on to her fork.

Siobhán had backed Helen up that morning when she'd suggested that Christina ask Mrs Kenny if she could move to their table in class. 'You've been looking a bit lonely with that empty space beside you since Áine left,' she'd pointed out. 'Ask, Christina. All she can say is no.'

Not wanting to get on the wrong side of Mrs Kenny, Christina had been reluctant to approach her, but the other two girls had kept at her and at her, until finally she'd given in, deciding it would probably be less of an ordeal to approach Mrs Kenny than to listen to both of them going on about it all day.

As she continued eating, Christina's thoughts were still on her two new companions. Although she found herself spending more time with them each day, she wasn't exactly comfortable with them just yet. There were little things about them that bothered her. Like the other day when they'd gone to the school shop at lunchtime. Siobhán had asked for two

Mars bars, and keeping one for herself, she'd handed the other one to Helen, saying to the girl behind the counter, 'She's paying.'

Christina had been surprised to see that Siobhán was pointing at her. Before she could protest, both girls had walked away. There was nothing Christina could do but hand over the money. Hurrying after the two of them, she'd said, 'Hey, come on Siobhán, pay up. That's the last of my pocket money gone for the week.'

But Siobhán had just looked straight at her and said coolly, 'Didn't you hear me? I said you were paying.' Christina listened in amazement as the other girl began talking about something completely different.

Christina had said no more about it then, but the next day when the three of them were in the shop, she'd said, 'OK, you can treat me today. I'll have a Mars, please.'

Siobhán had looked at her blankly and when Christina reminded her of what she'd done the day before, she said, 'I don't remember that, do you, Helen?'

To which Helen had replied, 'No, I don't remember either.'

And then there were the times when she said something that she considered intelligent and that made sense, and they both made her feel foolish with their smart answers. They were just so different to Áine. Áine was always the same, good-humoured, full of fun, easy to get on with. But then she couldn't expect everyone to be like Áine, she told herself briskly. Perhaps it was just a matter of getting to know the other two girls better. Anyway, whatever it was, she thought as she savoured the last mouthful of spaghetti sauce, today had been good fun. As soon as she'd helped her mother to wash up, she'd write to Áine and tell her all about it.

'Is that the pen you won?' Siobhán asked as Christina sat down beside her the next day, just as their history class was about to begin.

'Yes. Lovely, isn't it? It's one of those A.T. Cross sets.'

'Here, let's have a go,' Siobhán said, taking the pen from Christina's hand before she had time to say anything.

'Nice,' she said, after making a few doodles on the cover of her copybook. 'I think I'll borrow it for the rest of the day.'

Christina was about to protest but suddenly the class fell silent as Mr Conroy came into the room, laden down with books as usual.

'Siobhán,' Christina whispered, a little louder than she meant to. But after receiving a few sharp looks from the teacher she decided she'd better leave what she had to say until later. By breaktime, Siobhán still hadn't returned the pen and when Christina asked for it out in the school yard she just laughed and held it high above her head, teasing Christina, who was just that bit too short to reach it.

'Give it to me, Siobhán,' she begged eventually.

'Give it to me, Siobhán. Give it to me, Siobhán,' the other girl mimicked her, laughing.

'Now, now, Siobhán, don't be unkind to Áine's little Siamese twin,' Helen said, her pale face looking unusually pink as she arrived on the scene and joined in the teasing.

'*You* give it to her, then, if you care so much about her,' Siobhán said, tossing the pen quickly to Helen, who caught it expertly. But she didn't give it back to Christina either. Instead they both ran off to the other side of the school yard, still tossing the pen from one to the other.

When school finished for the day, Siobhán and Helen still had the pen in their possession. Christina watched them as they strolled down the school driveway together, arms entwined. They glanced back at her as they neared the end of it, and whispering something to each other, began laughing their heads off. Christina raced after them and once again demanded her pen back. One or two other girls glanced curiously at the three of them as they passed by, but it didn't seem to bother Siobhán, who replied sneeringly, 'Helen has it.'

But Helen just laughed and said, 'Siobhán has it,' when Christina asked her.

'It was only a joke,' Helen said next morning, when Christina threatened to tell Mrs Kenny what they'd done.

'There—there it is,' said Siobhán viciously, throwing the precious pen on to the desk in front of Christina. She picked it up and was about to put it back into its case when she noticed that the nib was bent.

'You've broken it, you've broken the nib,' she exclaimed.

'So? What if we have? Siobhán answered. 'What are you going to do about it? Go to dear Mrs Kenny and cry on her shoulder, will you? If you do, you'll be sorry. When we've finished with you, you'll wish you'd never won that stupid project competition. Won't she, Helen?' she asked, turning to her companion.

Something in her tone frightened Christina. She knew that the other girl was serious, that she would make her sorry if she spoke up. She didn't know how she would do it, but as Siobhán continued to stare at her, her dark eyes boring into her face, Christina knew she was capable of anything. And a look at Helen's sour face made her banish all thought of going to Mrs Kenny.

'You all right?' her mother asked her that evening as she noticed Christina sitting on the sofa staring into space.

There was no answer. Her daughter didn't appear to have heard the question.

'Christina,' she repeated.

'Sorry Mum, I was miles away.' Christina looked up apologetically.

'I was asking if you were all right. You've hardly said a word all night.'

'Oh yes, I'm fine, Mum. Just a bit tired. I think I'll go to bed shortly.'

'Good idea,' her mother agreed. 'Things were pretty hectic at work today for me, too. Think I'll have an early night myself,' she added, unplugging the TV and turning off the living room light.

Later as she lay in bed, staring into the darkness,

Christina wondered if perhaps she'd taken the whole thing too seriously. Had the pen business really been a joke? Was the broken nib an accident? Maybe she shouldn't have spoken so accusingly to Siobhán, maybe she should have given her time to explain what had happened, how it had been broken. She didn't really know. She was so used to being just with Áine and she hadn't mixed all that much with others girls. Maybe they did things like that to each other and didn't mean any harm. Even so, if it had all really been meant as a joke, Christina found it a strange one.

Oh well, she thought, trying to put the incident out of her mind in an effort to settle down to sleep, she'd just have to wait and see how things went the next day.

They were as nice as pie to her the next day. They didn't mention the pen and neither did Christina.

Chapter Three

The next couple of weeks passed happily enough for Christina. The class was now well settled into the autumn term. Second year seemed to bring a lot of extra homework with it and there were weary groans each day as the girls noted down what had to be done. True to her promise, Áine wrote each week, long, newsy letters all about the farm, school and village life. From what she wrote it seemed to Christina that the workload at St Columcille's wasn't any less than at St Mary's. But what was keeping the girls in Christina's class going right now was the thought of the half-term disco.

'You going?' Siobhán asked one afternoon on the way home.

'Maybe. It depends...' Christina replied.

'On what?'

'Well, last year I went with Áine.'

'So, this year you can come with us, can't she, Helen?' Siobhán offered generously.

'Sure,' Helen agreed readily. What's it like, this disco. Is it any good?'

'Oh, that's right. You weren't there last year. I'd forgotten you only moved into Glenwood half-way through first year,' Siobhán said.

'I really enjoyed it last year anyway,' Christina assured Helen.

'Me too,' added Siobhán. 'Even though Mrs Kenny seemed to be everywhere I looked,' she said with a laugh.

'Áine says they're having one at St Columcille's as

well,' Christina said.

At the mention of Áine's name, Siobhán's mood seemed to change. 'Oh no, here we go again,' she said sneeringly to Christina. 'All you ever talk about is Áine, Áine, Áine.'

'No I don't.'

'Yes, you do. You know, I could never stand that girl. I don't know why you and half the school thought she was so great,' Siobhán snapped. 'Tell me, did it hurt?'

'Did what hurt?' Christina asked,.

'The operation to separate the pair of you.'

'What a horrible thing to say. Don't you realise you shouldn't joke about something like that,' Christina replied, unable to keep the anger and disgust out of her voice.

'Ah, forget it,' Siobhán said, her mood changing again just as quickly. 'So that's a date then. The three of us will go together to the disco. All we've got to do now is decide what we're going to wear.'

The evenings grew shorter as September passed. October arrived, the nights drawing in earlier and earlier. It was on one such dark evening, as Christina sat in her bedroom doing her homework, that the telephone rang. Engrossed in a difficult maths question, she jumped as its shrill ringing penetrated the stillness of the house.

Probably Mum, she thought, as she ran downstairs to answer it.

As she lifted the receiver, she hoped that her mother wasn't ringing to say she'd be delayed at the office. It had happened a couple of times lately and

Christina found these dark evenings long enough as it was.

'Hello.'

There was no answer at first, so Christina spoke again, this time raising her voice a little. 'Hello, is that you, Mum?'

'Crees-teen-a,' she heard a voice say huskily. 'Is that you, Crees-teen-a?'

'Yes. Who's that?'

'Crees-teen-a, we know you're alone,' the voice said, 'and we're coming to get you.'

'Who is it, who is it?' Christina asked again, her voice beginning to shake. 'What do you want?'

But there was no reply, just a click at the other end of the line. Whoever it was had hung up.

Christina was trembling as she replaced the receiver. The house seemed to have grown suddenly darker, as though the October evening was in a hurry to give way to the night, and she felt very frightened. She went from room to room, drawing the curtains and turning on all the lights. In the kitchen, she checked to see that the French windows were securely locked, all the time praying that her mother would come home soon.

She tried to settle back down to her homework, but couldn't. She couldn't get the phone call out of her mind. What would she do if they rang again, she wondered, becoming even more upset at the thought. Surely they wouldn't do it a second time…Quickly heading downstairs again she picked up the phone and dialled her mother's office number. She had to talk to her. She'd tell her what she should do. It seemed an age before the switchboard operator

41

answered.

'Mrs Miles? I'm sorry, she's at a meeting at the moment, I'm afraid she can't be disturbed unless it's really important,' she said to Christina. 'But I can take a message and give it to her when she's free, if you like,' she added kindly, recognising Christina's voice.

'No, thank you. It doesn't matter,' Christina said, and hung up.

When the phone rang again about half an hour later, at first she wasn't going to answer it, but then she decided she would. Maybe the switchboard operator had told her mother that she'd called even though she hadn't actually asked her to. Maybe it really was her mother this time. Nervously she lifted the receiver.

'Mum?' she said, her voice barely audible.

But it wasn't her mother.

'You're still alone, aren't you?' She heard the same husky voice. 'We know you are and we're coming to get you, Crees-teen-a, we're really coming this time.'

'Stop it, stop it, whoever you are,' Christina pleaded, now terror-stricken. 'Leave me alone, please leave me alone.'

There was an abrupt click and again the mysterious caller was gone, but not before Christina heard a shrill laugh at the other end of the line. Something about the laugh seemed familiar to her, and as she stood there, still holding the receiver in her hand, she suddenly knew who that laugh belonged to.

Siobhán. It was Siobhán.

That was exactly the way she laughed.

She said nothing about the phone calls to her mother when she finally arrived home from work that evening. Frightening as they'd been at the time, now that she knew who'd been behind them, she felt somewhat embarrassed at having to admit that she'd been scared silly by someone she knew!

Siobhán's face next morning told Christina nothing. She greeted her in an extremely friendly manner and Christina began to think she might have been mistaken about the laugh. How could the other girl be so friendly towards her now, she wondered, puzzled, if she'd acted so maliciously only the evening before. During the day she even reminded Christina of the fact that they'd agreed to go to the disco together in a couple of weeks' time. Christina was filled with doubts about the whole episode, but within days any doubts she'd had as to who'd made the phone calls were quickly dispelled.

Along with History, English was Christina's favourite subject. Mrs Kenny was always on about how they should "read, read, read" and did all she could to instill a love of books into her pupils. A bit like Gay Byrne, as Áine used to joke. According to her mother, who was an avid listener to his programme every morning on the radio, he regularly advocated that parents encourage their children to learn to appreciate good books at as young an age as possible. The class had English every day, and, while some of the girls bemoaned the fact, Christina looked forward to it and was never happier than when their teacher set them an essay to write. According to Christina's mother, her daughter had inherited her love of reading and writing from her father.

Now, for the second time during English class that morning, Christina searched systematically through every book in her schoolbag. A creature of habit, she was sure she had put it in, but where on earth was it, she wondered.

'Have you seen my English copybook, by any chance?' she whispered to Helen, who was busily writing beside her. Helen shook her head.

'Siobhán, did you see it?'

'No, and you'd better be quiet. Mrs Kenny's not in the best of form today,' Siobhán warned her. 'If she catches you talking, we'll all suffer.'

Christina began rummaging through her things again, although she suspected it was a waste of time. She knew that Mrs Kenny wanted the essays in the next morning at the latest, as they'd had since last week to write them. If she couldn't find hers, it meant she'd have to write it out all over again—if she could remember any of it. And this evening, too, on top of all her other homework! What a mess, she thought, as she finally gave up searching. She'd put a lot of effort into that particular essay and was convinced it was one of the best she'd written so far this term. Pity she'd mislaid it. It wasn't like her to lose things, but still, maybe it was at home somewhere. She wouldn't give up until she'd had a good look there, too.

It was a lovely bright October morning. Golden and russet autumn leaves were scattered on the pavements and Christina kicked carelessly at one or two of them as she walked along. As she reached the school entrance and turned into the driveway, a gentle breeze curled through the branches of the trees and sent dozens more of the crisp leaves swirling to the ground. Half-way through October already, Christina thought, as she brushed away a leaf which had clung to the sleeve of her coat. Only two more weeks until half-term, and half-term meant the school disco. There was nothing else talked about amongst her classmates as the date drew nearer. Like her, quite a few of the girls in her year weren't allowed to go to discos during the school term, so for them it was an extra-exciting event. As well as the usual deejay, they'd heard that some local boys who'd recently formed their own group had agreed to play during the interval. So it looked as though this year's disco was going to be even better than last time.

Even though it was still a fortnight away, she and Helen and Siobhán had already agreed what time they'd meet and Siobhán had told Helen and Christina that her mother would collect the three of them when the disco was over and drive the other two girls home. Christina smiled to herself. She was really looking forward to it and, today being Friday, as usual she was looking forward to the weekend because it meant two full, leisurely days at home with her mother.

All in all, she was in an extremely happy mood as the English class was called to order.

'Girls, girls, settle down now, please,' Mrs Kenny directed, pausing for a moment or two until there was complete silence. 'I've had a chance to go through the essays which I took up the other day and I must say I was very pleased with the standard of writing.'

She smiled as she looked around the room.

'I picked out the three essays that I decided are the best and thought it might be interesting if the girls who wrote them each read out a little of their work. All right?'

A murmer of interested surprise went around the room. This was something Mrs Kenny hadn't done before.

'I've chosen those written by Margaret O'Brien, Lavinia Walsh and Siobhán O'Dwyer. Please come up and collect your work, girls.'

As Siobhán stood up, Helen gave her a congratulatory clap on the back. Christina mouthed the words 'well done,' and then sat back with the rest of the class to listen to the girls read. She'd been a little disappointed when her own name hadn't been amongst the three called, but as she listened to first Margaret and then Lavinia read, she had to admit that their essays were much better than what she'd managed in her second, rather rushed, effort. But the essay she'd lost had been every bit as good as what they'd just read, of that she had no doubt. What a pity she hadn't been able to hand it up, she thought again, still wondering what could have happened to it.

Siobhán was last to read.

Christina thought she must be imagining it at first, but as Siobhán continued, she knew that her imagination wasn't playing tricks on her. It wasn't the first time she'd heard what was being read. No, she'd read those words out loud herself only a few days before, after she'd finished writing them. So that was what had happened. She hadn't mislaid it at all. Siobhán had taken her exercise book and copied every word of her work and was now presenting it as her own. Of all the underhand things to do, Christina thought, anger welling up inside her as she looked up to where the other girl stood, coolly accepting the loud applause of her classmates, her dark eyes gleaming with pleasure, her short, shiny hair framing her face, looking as though butter wouldn't melt in her mouth. And she'd been so friendly recently that Christina had almost convinced herself she'd been mistaken about the identity of the person who'd made the frightening phone call, while all the time, behind her back, she'd been laughing at her and planning this. And looking across to where Helen sat, smirking all over her pasty face, Christina felt in no doubt that Siobhán hadn't acted alone. No, Helen had been part of it too.

'That was my essay you read out,' Christina whispered accusingly to Siobhán as soon as she sat down. Siobhán looked at her with raised eyebrows.

'Your essay? What're you talking about?'

'You know very well. You took my exercise book and copied my essay. How could you be so mean? How could you take praise for it when you knew it wasn't your own work?' Christina asked angrily.

'Quiet! Quiet, girls,' Mrs Kenny said, looking in Christina's direction. 'You can do all your talking at breaktime.'

Christina immediately fell silent but determined to

47

have it out with Siobhán later. She wasn't going to let her away with this.

'Prove it then, prove it,' Siobhán taunted viciously. The three of them stood in a corner of the schoolyard, Christina between the other two, her face flushed and angry.

'Show us your essay and let's see if it's the same,' Helen joined in, siding with her friend as usual.

'When you give me back my copybook, I will,' Christina told them, almost on the verge of tears.

'Give you back your copybook! What copybook? We haven't got your copybook. Have we got her copybook, Helen?' Siobhán asked, looking innocently at Helen, who was standing there with a sickly grin on her face.

Fighting to keep back her tears, Christina swung round to Helen, demanding angrily, 'Look, Helen, did she take it or didn't she? I know you know what happened?'

For a second, Christina had the feeling that Helen was slightly taken aback by her sudden attack. But she quickly recovered, taking Siobhán by the arm. 'Ah come on, leave her. She doesn't know what she's talking about.'

They walked off, leaving Christina standing there alone, knowing she'd lost. They were right, of course. She couldn't prove anything. Without her copybook it was her word against Siobhán's. And if Helen followed her usual pattern, she'd back Siobhán up till the very end, maybe even say they'd been together when Siobhán had written the essay. How could their teacher decide who was telling the truth and who wasn't without some form of proof?

No, the only hope would be the copybook and it didn't take a genius to know that Siobhán and Helen would make sure that she never set eyes on it again.

The bell rang, signalling the end of break. Despondently, Christina joined the other girls as they filed back into class. She was oblivious of the chatter around her, so deep was she in her own thoughts. The lovely October day had been completely spoiled. Now she wanted it to be over as quickly as possible, not because it was Friday and the weekend was coming up, not because she'd have two whole days to spend with her mother. She wanted it to be over simply to get away from the two of them.

Although she tried hard, Christina couldn't hide the fact that something was wrong when her mother arrived home that evening.

'You look a bit fed up, love,' her mother commented, noticing her long face. 'Something wrong at school?'

'Not really,' Christina replied, sorely tempted to pour out all that had happened.

'Come on, now. I know you better than that,' said her mother. 'Tell me what's bothering you.'

'Oh, it was just that essay I told you about. Remember?'

'The one you couldn't find, the one you were especially pleased with?'

'Yes.'

'Well?' her mother prompted.

'Well, my second attempt obviously wasn't much good, because Mrs Kenny chose the three best essays today and mine wasn't one of them.'

'Ah now, that's not like you, not able to take a beating.' Her mother put her arm around her, looking at her in surprise.

'It's not just that, Mum, it's…' But Christina didn't finish. Noticing a strained look on her mother's face, she bit back what she'd been about to say. Angela Miles looked tired and drawn, having obviously had another difficult day at the agency. There was no point in telling her the whole sorry tale and burdening her with *her* problems too, Christina thought dismally. She knew her mother was finding it tough going, working and running a home at the same time, and that she worried about leaving her on her own so much. 'The ratrace,' she sometimes joked, 'has speeded up a lot since I was last part of it. You know, I have to try really hard to keep up with all that's happening, There was a time when a girl could bury herself away in a nice quiet corner of the accounts department, but not any more, I'm afraid.'

'Tell you what,' her mother was saying now, 'you can stay up a bit later than usual. After all it's Friday and we don't have to get up early in the morning. We'll see if there's anything good on TV and,' she added, 'we'll spoil ourselves a bit, too. We'll go down to the Chinese take-away and you can pick whatever you fancy for supper. Maybe that'll cheer you up. How about it?'

Christina forced herself to smile.

Poor Mum, always trying to do her best. No, there was no point in worrying her. What could she do, anyway? Siobhán and Helen were far too clever.

Over the weekend Christina thought a lot about what

had happened. She couldn't understand why they were treating her so cruelly. She'd done nothing to deserve their taunts and sly tricks. She knew from Siobhán's earlier threat that if she went to Mrs Kenny they'd probably just make life even more difficult for her. But she would ask her teacher if she could move back to her old seat in class, make some excuse about not being able to see the board. After that, she vowed, she'd keep as far away as possible from both of them. If she had nothing to do with them, she reasoned, they could do nothing to her!

Chapter Four

Keeping clear of Siobhán and Helen wasn't as easy as she thought it would be. On the following Monday morning when Christina arrived into the classroom, she was surprised to find Miss Furlong in charge.

'Mrs Kenny has phoned in to say she's been laid low with some sort of bug, so I'll be sitting in for her today,' Miss Furlong announced, a slightly harrassed note in her voice. This didn't encourage Christina to broach the subject of changing places. She decided it would be best to leave it for the moment and took her usual seat beside the other two girls. She neither looked at nor spoke to them as she did so and, to her relief, neither of them said anything to her either. She continued to ignore them as the morning progressed and in the yard, too, she kept to herself. But to her dismay, she realised that they seemed to see her aloofness as simply another reason to torment her. After a few minutes they came and stood beside her, giving her sidelong glances and then giggling and whispering to each other.

'How's the romance?' Siobhán asked, suddenly taking a step nearer to her.

Christina didn't answer, not knowing what she meant.

'All off, is it? Mum doesn't like him any more, does she?' she said, her voice loaded with sarcasm.

'What are you talking about?' Christina asked.

'You mean you don't know?'

'Know what?' Christina asked, curious despite herself.

'That your mother's got a boyfriend.'

'A what?'

'Boyfriend. You do know what the word means, don't you?'

'Don't be ridiculous, my mother hasn't got any boyfriend.'

'Not that she's told *you* about, you mean.'

Christina's voice rose slightly. 'I said she hasn't got a boyfriend. Of course I'd know if she had.'

'Well, there's no need to shout about it. But we know better, don't we, Helen?' Siobhán asked, turning to her companion.

'Yeah, that's right. She gets out of his car just past Siobhán's house a couple of evenings each week. Maroon, isn't it, Siobhán?'

'Something like that. Big expensive-looking thing. Must be nice to be driven home from work in such luxury.'

'I don't believe either of you,' Christina said angrily, but they could see she was shaken.

Encouraged by their success, Siobhán went on. 'Ask her then, and see who's right. I would, if I were you. Before you find you've got yourself a stepfather,' she finished with a laugh.

Christina moved away but they followed her and continued their giggling and whispering and later, during Civics, they passed notes to each other and stared at her, unblinking, every chance they got. She began to feel very ill-at-ease under their constant scrutiny, and at times even a little frightened. She was really glad when the day finally came to an end.

That evening as she tried to do her homework, she kept thinking of what they'd said. She insisted to herself that she didn't believe a word of it, but at the back of her mind she guiltily had to admit there was just a trace of doubt. Her mother hadn't mentioned getting a lift home from work, but she had been late home a few times lately. She never went into much detail about what delayed her when she arrived, just saying that something came up at the office, before starting straight into preparing a meal for both of them. And until now, Christina had never thought to ask what had kept her!

Had she been meeting some man for an hour or so after work before coming home? Had she been getting out of his car elsewhere in Glenwood so her daughter wouldn't know what was going on? Christina remembered one morning about a week ago when she'd noticed her mother taking extra special care with her appearance before setting off for work.

'One of the girls is leaving today and we're all going out to lunch,' she'd said to Christina by way of explanation.

But was that the truth? Had she really been going out with her workmates?

What if what Siobhán and Helen had said was really true, and her mother had found someone she'd grown fond of? If she decided to get married again, everything would change completely. Christina remembered Áine once telling her about an American cousin who was about the same age as herself. Her parents were divorced and her mother had married again. 'I hate her new husband,' she told Áine when she was over in Dublin on holiday. 'If I didn't get to spend one weekend a month with Dad, I think I'd go crazy.' Well at least the American girl still had her father to go to, Christina thought sadly. If her own mother married again, she wouldn't even have that consolation. Would they have to move somewhere else? Maybe her mother's boyfriend had a house of his own and he'd expect them to live there. How she'd hate to have to leave St Mary's and everything that was familiar to her. Stop it, stop it, Christina told herself angrily. You're beginning to believe them already. It's not true, it just isn't true.

Opening her maths book, Christina tried to concentrate, feeling ashamed of herself for thinking such things about her mother. She knew she wouldn't go behind her back like that. After all, she was free and entitled to see anyone she liked and there was no need for her to be secretive about it. Siobhán was lying, Christina just knew it.

The behaviour of Siobhán and Helen followed the same pattern as the days passed, and although Christina held her head high and tried to ignore them, she found it harder and harder as the week went on.

She did her best to mix with other people in class but nearly everyone had special close friends already and she always seemed to find herself on the periphery of whatever was going on.

If only Áine hadn't had to go away. If only Mr O'Neill hadn't lost his job. If only her own father hadn't died, her mother wouldn't have had to go out to work, and there'd be no talk of her having a boyfriend. As Christina lay in bed each night thinking about it all, it seemed to her that everyone she'd ever loved and depended on had either gone away or was busy doing something else. Most nights she cried herself to sleep, making sure that her mother didn't hear her sobs, although sometimes she almost wished she *would* hear. Then maybe she'd give in and tell her everything that was going on, maybe even find the courage to ask her if what they were saying was true. Some nights she found it impossible to sleep at all, the sound of Siobhán's and Helen's jeering voices chanting, 'boyfriend, stepfather, boyfriend, stepfather,' over and over, jolting her back into wakefulness again and again.

It was the longest, loneliest week of her life.

Now more than ever, Christina looked forward to Áine's letters.

'The school here is much farther away than St Mary's. I travel to it each day on the school bus,' she'd written in her latest letter.

It collects us in the morning at the end of the boreen leading up to the farm and leaves us back home in the evenings. It's great crack, especially if you get a seat up front behind the driver. Our regular driver's called Johnny. He's a real Jekyll and Hyde, one minute telling jokes and playing tricks on people but if he has to wait a minute for you, he goes mad altogether. As Thomas says, 'the way he uses that horn, anyone would think he got it from Santa for Christmas.' Trust Thomas! Everyone around here knows everyone else. In that way it's different from Dublin but much more friendly. I'd rather be back there but on the other hand I'm enjoying it in Castledonagh, too. Our visits to Granny and Grandad were always so short and now, because we're together all the time, I'm getting to know them in a way I'd never have been able to if we'd just kept

coming on holiday. Granny is really a great character.
Naturally, having been born and bred here, she knows
everyone, and I mean everyone, and everything about
them. And the stories she tells! Christina, I just couldn't
manage to put them all on paper, but when we get together
I'll fill you in on some of them. Gráinne's terrific, too. I'm
sure you'd like her. When the summer comes, maybe your
mother will let you come down to stay for a while and then
the three of us can be together.

Christina's eyes filled with tears as she read the letter
over and over, her eyes drawn each time to the
postscript where Áine had written '*Enjoy the disco.*'

Half-term was only days away and the way things
were, there was no chance now that she would be
going to the disco. Even if she managed to team up
with some of her other classmates at the last minute,
she knew her two tormentors would be there and
with both of them hovering all night, it wouldn't be
any fun. All the time she'd been hoping they'd
apologise for what they'd done with her essay and
that things would finally be all right. But only
yesterday as they'd passed her in the corridor she'd
heard Siobhán remark in a loud voice, obviously
meant for her to hear, 'I can't wait for the disco—and
to think we almost made the mistake of planning to
go with you know who.'

Helen had nodded as Siobhán continued. 'She's
such an eejit, you know. Even though she denied it, I
could see she swallowed that story about her mother
having a boyfriend.'

Equally loudly Helen replied, 'Well, anyone that
thick deserves to be made a fool of.' Then, throwing a

sidelong glance in Christina's direction, she added, 'Not mentioning anybody in particular, of course.'

Thinking of it now, Christina could still feel her cheeks burning at the realisation that they'd made a complete fool of her, that they'd made up the whole story about her mother, and that all her worrying and guilty doubts had been for nothing.

Christina hadn't said anything yet to her mother about not going to the disco. An hour or so before she was supposed to be meeting Helen and Siobhán, she planned to develop a sick stomach and say she felt far too ill to go. The thought of the four long, lonely days of half-term depressed her and once half-term was over, there was nothing to look forward to but going back to the awful situation at school.

The strain of the situation, coupled with lack of sleep, was beginning to show in Christina's performance at school and a few times she came in for quite severe criticism from her teachers, Mrs Kenny in particular. Then one day something happened which made her forget all about the tough front she'd been putting up. During the five-minute break between Geography and Science classes, Christina went into the cloakroom and found herself face to face with Siobhán. The other girl was standing in one of the cubicles with the door wide open and Christina was about to turn and walk out again when she noticed that Siobhán was clutching her stomach with one hand, while she held the other across her mouth. She was extremely pale, and, thinking she was going to faint, Christina, for the moment forgetting her own feelings, moved swiftly to her side and put her arm around her shoulders.

'Siobhán, what's wrong? Are you all right?'

But Siobhán had no opportunity to answer. Almost instantly she gave a low moan and began to retch violently. Christina held her until the spasm passed and, when she had recovered a little, took her over to an old armchair in the corner of the room. Siobhán flopped into it gratefully, resting her head against the back, while Christina went to fill a glass with water.

'Here, drink this while I open the window a bit wider. You'll feel much better with a breath of fresh air.'

It was only as the fresh air began to filter in that Christina realised what had caused Siobhán to be sick. She noticed that there was a strong smell of smoke in the cloakroom and that it had been even stronger in the confined space of the cubicle they'd just come out of.

Siobhán had been smoking! The stupid girl had only herself to blame for what had happened, she thought, as she watched her take a sip of water. She'd been breaking the rules and now if Christina was caught in here with her, with the smell of smoke still hanging in the air, she could be accused of doing exactly the same thing. Not only was it against the rules to smoke in school, but if you were caught smoking outside school while wearing the school uniform, you'd be in big trouble too. Christina started to move towards the door, fanning the air as she did so. Siobhán had caused her enough problems already. She wasn't going to hang around and have one of the teachers walk in and find them together. Realising that Christina knew what she'd been up to,

Siobhán said, 'You wouldn't snitch on me, would you?'

Obviously taking her silence as consent, Siobhán went on, 'You're a real friend, Christina, a real friend.'

Christina stared at her in amazement.

Her face still pale, but smiling sweetly, Siobhán was looking at her as if the events of the past weeks had never happened, as if all the snide remarks and stifled giggles had been a figment of Christina's imagination, as if they had always been 'real friends'!

As Christina hurried home from school that afternoon, Siobhán and Helen caught up with her.

'Thanks for this morning, Christina,' Siobhán said breathlessly. 'Now I'll collect what belongs to me, if you don't mind.'

Christina looked at her. 'What do you mean?'

'Just what I said, I'll have what belongs to me,' she repeated.

'But I haven't got anything belonging to you.'

'You'd be surprised. Isn't that right?' Siobhán said to Helen and they both began to laugh. 'It's in the left-hand pocket of your coat, if I remember rightly,' Siobhán said, pointing.

Still mystified, Christina put her hand into her pocket.

'Well, wasn't I right?' grinned Siobhán, as Christina pulled out a half-empty packet of cigarettes which the other girl grabbed out of her hand.

'Sorry, but I couldn't take a chance on being caught. I thought Old Kenny was looking at me very peculiarly when I came back from break this morning.'

'So you slipped them into my pocket. What about me being caught? Didn't you think about that at all?'

Siobhán looked at her, all innocence. 'But Christina, you'd only have to bat your big blue eyes at her and all would be forgiven,' she said coyly before she and Helen flounced away.

Speechless, Christina looked after them, thinking that Siobhán must be the most selfish girl she'd ever known. A bit further down the road Helen and Siobhán stopped and a second or two later Christina saw the flare from a match as Siobhán lit a cigarette and brazenly began smoking it.

After the incident in the cloakroom, Siobhán and Helen's treatment of Christina changed dramatically. All their jeering and teasing stopped. Although she still sat beside them, having abandoned her resolve to ask to be moved back to her old seat, she was still extremely wary of them and continued to have as little as possible to do with them. But at times they went out of their way to be friendly towards her and on these occasions she felt a glimmer of hope that at some stage in the future she might even be able to bring herself to trust them again. For the moment she was happy enough to feel like her old self, to be able to look forward once more to school each day, and to sleep from the time her head hit the pillow until the alarm clock awakened her rudely each morning. She was managing to get back into the swing of her schoolwork now too, and Mrs Kenny could no longer find fault with her. Apart from the fact that Áine was not around, Christina couldn't have asked for things to be better.

Chapter Five

Patricia Doran sat in front of Christina for most classes. From being a girl of average height, she had grown rapidly during the summer holidays and she was head and shoulders over the rest of the class when they came back in September. As a result, she went around most of the time with her shoulders hunched, in an effort to look less conspicuous. She was an extremely quiet girl, so quiet in fact that it was an effort to make conversation with her. So Christina was rather surprised when, late one afternoon during Mrs Kenny's English class, Patricia turned around and whispered to her that she'd completely forgotten to tell her that Mr Doyle wanted to see her.

'I'm really sorry, Christina. I forgot all about it.'

'Before lunch? But that was ages ago,' Christina whispered back, keeping an eye on Mrs Kenny as she wrote their homework on the board.

'You can blame it on me. Tell him I forgot to tell you. Go on, don't worry, I'll write down your homework for you,' she added generously, finishing what Christina thought must have been the longest sentence she'd ever heard her speak.

Christina slipped quietly from her seat and, approaching her teacher, quickly explained her reason for wanting to leave the room.

'Hurry along then,' Mrs Kenny replied. 'Oh, and take all your effects with you. The classroom door will probably be locked by the time you've finished.'

Christina nodded as she packed up her things.

'And don't forget to get the homework from

someone,' her teacher reminded her as she left the room.

Racing down the length of the corridor, she stopped short when she reached the headmaster's office. Her heart was thumping. She wondered why he wanted to see her. He didn't usually give what the girls called 'a private audience' unless there was some reason for it. Nine times out of ten the reason was trouble. She crossed her fingers and gave a timid knock.

'Come in,' she heard Mr Doyle call. Taking a deep breath, she turned the handle and stepped into his room. Every available inch of space seemed to be occupied by books or papers of one sort or another. The desk behind which the headmaster now sat had innumerable files spread all over it and the phone was only partially visible, propping up his copy of the morning newspaper. Christina remembered Áine once describing Mr Doyle's office as 'organised chaos.'

Paddy Doyle's own appearance also had a cluttered look about it. Not only had he about half a dozen pens sticking out of the top pocket of his sports jacket, but there was a biro stuck behind his right ear. Christina wondered how anyone could need so many pens.

'Ah, Christina Miles, child. Conas atá tú?' the headmaster greeted her, breaking in on her thoughts. 'What can I do for you?' he asked pleasantly.

'Pardon?'

'I asked what I could do for you, child?' he repeated patiently.

'I...eh, I was told you wanted to see me, Mr Doyle.'

Christina's face reddened as she spoke.

'Did I, now? I don't think so,' he said, puzzled. 'And who told you that?'

'Oh, just one of the girls,' Christina said vaguely, not wanting to mention Patricia by name. 'But she must have been mistaken,' she mumbled, moving back towards the door, anxious to get away.

'Yes, she must have. Well, off you go and tell whoever it was to save that kind of thing up for April fool's day in future,' he said, not unkindly.

'But I could have sworn I heard him mention your name. I was passing along the corridor as he was talking to Mr Johnson and I'm sure I heard him say he wanted to see you,' Patricia assured Christina later as they walked down the school driveway together. 'Hope he wasn't mad at you,' she added contritely.

'No, he was OK but I felt a terrible fool. It was really embarrassing. Oh by the way, did you remember to write down my English homework for me?'

'Yes, I told you I would. Here it is.' And Patricia handed Christina a piece of paper folded in two.

'Thanks,' Christina said, slipping it into her pocket. 'See you tomorrow, then.' She and Patricia went their separate ways.

'I'm surprised at Mrs Kenny giving that amount of homework, I really am,' her mother remarked when she arrived home after six o'clock that evening and found Christina still working and less than half-way through what she had to do. She looked into the oven, then turned to her daughter and said in an exasperated tone, 'You didn't even turn it on! The casserole is stone-cold.'

'Oh sorry, Mum. I was so busy, I completely forgot about it. It's all this homework, you see...'

'I know, I know, love. I'm sorry, too. It's just that I'm exhausted and I was looking forward to coming home to something tasty and then putting my feet up. I've had nothing but hassle at work. And Mr Moore—you know the new head of my department I told you about—well, he's turning out to be very awkward. So,' she said with a sigh, 'it seems we've both had a hard day. Look, don't worry, I'll put on some sausages and chips. They won't take too long and we can have the casserole tomorrow. But first of all, I'll run upstairs and get out of this suit.'

As she went upstairs, Angela Miles couldn't help thinking that it just wasn't good enough. All that homework and the poor child looked so tired. If she was getting that much study to do now, what would things be like next year when she was preparing for Junior Cert.

Lately she'd been worried about Christina. She had a feeling there was something bothering her, especially that evening a few weeks ago when she'd found her sitting on the sofa brooding. She hadn't seemed to want to talk then; she'd made some excuse about being tired and had gone to bed early. Surely she'd confide in her if there was something wrong. They'd always been able to talk easily to each other. Coming up to the mid-term break she'd seemed particularly quiet and of course getting ill at the last minute on the night of the disco and not being able to go hadn't helped. Still, she seemed to have perked up quite a bit since then. Maybe it was simply that Christina had been missing Áine a lot during the first half-term at school without her and that now she'd find it easier to adjust. She was lucky that Siobhán and Helen had befriended her so quickly, although now that she thought about it, Christina hadn't mentioned them very much lately. She'd noticed too that Christina wasn't very happy if she was delayed in getting home from work. Not that she blamed her. She spent long enough on her own each afternoon until she came in. She'd just have to keep an eye on things, find a bit more time for her. But, she thought wearily, time seemed to be in very short supply these days, what with rushing out to work in the morning and rushing home to cook meals in the evening.

As she hung up her jacket and skirt, she reflected that it was no joke trying to be both mother and father to a teenage girl. Lord, how she missed Brian, missed him every day of her life, but especially on days like today.

It was really cold. Even with the central heating going full blast, the classroom didn't feel all that warm. Christina glanced out of the window at the cold, lifeless, grey sky and gave a slight shiver. By the look of things, it was going to be pretty chilly walking home today.

As the class began packing up fifteen minutes later, to Christina's surprise, Mrs Kenny signalled to her. 'Don't go for a minute, will you?' she said. ' I'd like to see you after class.'

As soon as the room was cleared, the teacher

71

motioned to her to come up beside her desk. All sorts of things flashed through Christina's mind as she made her way up the room, but she had no real idea what all this might be about. She was relieved to see that Mrs. Kenny wasn't wearing her 'thunderous' expression, as the girls called it, so it couldn't be all that bad.

'So your mother's at work now, I hear, Christina,' her year-head began.

'Yes, that's right.'

'And that means you must spend quite a bit of time alone, I suppose.'

'Well…yes.'

'Plenty of time for study, so?'

Christina nodded, wondering where the conversation was leading.

'And that's the very reason I wanted to talk to you,' Mrs Kenny went on. 'I'm all in favour of plenty of study, dear, but overdoing it can be harmful too, you know. Your work did fall off for a while there just before half-term, but you're well up to standard again now. So my advice to you, Christina, is to take up a hobby of some sort if you've time on your hands. You know the old saying: All work and no play…'

Christina didn't answer. She was completely at a loss to know what her teacher was getting at. Mrs Kenny saw how mystified she was and said, 'I'm talking about the other night, of course, Christina. Don't you realise you did twice the amount of homework I gave you?'

Christina frowned, trying to make some sense out of what she had heard. Twice the amount of homework? What did she mean? She'd done exactly what Patricia had copied down for her. *What Patricia had copied down*, she repeated silently, all at once realising the cruel trick that had been played on her. She knew now that Patricia had purposely lied about Mr Doyle wanting to see her. She'd made it all up to get Christina out of the way so that she had an opportunity to write down the 'homework'. What's more, Christina had a pretty good idea who'd put her up to it!

Mrs Kenny was still speaking. 'Ease up on yourself, child. By all means do your work, but leave it to me to decide how much. All right? Now, off you go and remember what I said.'

Christina ran all the way home, completely unaware of the cold breeze and the ominous grey sky. She managed to hold back the tears until she closed the hall door behind her, but then harsh, bitter sobs burst from her, filling the hallway, drowning out the loud ticking of the clock. Siobhán and Helen, Helen and Siobhán—their names pounded away inside her head. She had no doubt that they were behind all this. Just as she'd begun to trust them once more, they'd done it again. Now they'd recruited Patricia into their ranks, Patricia whom she'd hardly ever had anything to do with and who had no reason in the world to treat her like this.

Was she now to be suspicious of all her classmates? Why were they treating her like this, she asked herself for the thousandth time. What did I do, anyway, a voice inside her kept saying. But she could find no answer to the question.

Christina suddenly sat up in bed. The thought of having to go to school in the morning and see the smug faces of Siobhán and Helen was unbearable. If only she'd talked to her mother in the beginning. But she couldn't do that now, she knew; she'd left it too late. Her mother was under a lot of strain at the moment. Not only was she trying to cope with problems at work, she was still grieving for Dad. Christina knew that only too well from the sadness in her voice whenever she mentioned his name. No, lumping it all on her mother just wasn't on. Maybe she should have confided in Mrs Kenny but she'd no proof of the things they'd done. It would be their word against hers, and now with Patricia involved there would be three of them. She had to do something; she couldn't take any more. But what, she agonised, as she shifted restlessly, clenching and unclenching the soft duvet-cover in her hands.

And then to her amazement it came to her, and she almost laughed with relief. She wondered why she hadn't thought of it before. At last, at long last, she knew exactly what she had to do.

Chapter Six

The train to Westport pulled out of Heuston Station at one o'clock. Christina heaved a sigh of relief, having waited all morning for this moment.

It had been so late the previous night when she'd decided what to do that there was no chance to find out what time the first train would be leaving. By the time her mother had gone to work that morning and she'd had a chance to phone Iarnród Éireann, the early train was already on its way. And then, of course, there'd been the question of the money for her ticket. She knew her mother always took her handbag upstairs with her at night and left it on the bedside locker. But she hadn't dared to go in during the night to take something from her purse. She'd had to wait until this morning when her mother was in the shower. Christina had felt terrible, just like a thief, as she'd taken the twenty-pound note and slipped it up the sleeve of her school jumper. That was something else she'd had to remember, to dress in her school uniform, so as not to arouse her mother's suspicions. After she'd left for work, Christina had quickly taken her schoolbooks from her bag and packed instead her anorak, sweatshirt and jeans. She'd decided it would be best to leave the house at the uual time, wearing her uniform, just in case she bumped into any of the neighbours. She wanted everything to appear as normal as possible.

As soon as she got off the bus in Talbot Street, she headed up towards Clery's in O'Connell Street, where she went directly to the ladies cloakroom. In the cramped space she changed out of her uniform and donned her casual clothes. Then, putting her uniform into her bag, she opened the door cautiously, making sure that the cloakroom attendant wasn't paying her any attention, and headed out again into the main part of the shop. She knew she'd quite a few hours to kill before setting off in the direction of the quays and up to the station, and she was hoping she wouldn't bump into anyone she knew. If she did, however, she planned to say she was in town for a dental appointment and was window-shopping until it was time to meet up with her mother.

The morning had seemed endless but now, at last, she was on her way. Christina took from her bag a book that she'd bought secondhand that morning in Chapters, and slipping a little further down in her seat, she opened it and tried to read. But her thoughts were in turmoil.

The pages of the book blurred as tears welled up, misting her eyes. Christina knew that by taking this journey she was going to inflict great unhappiness on someone she dearly loved. She knew her mother would be frantic with worry when she got home from work late that evening and found her gone. She'd left a note saying that she had to go away for a while, although not saying where, and begging her mother to believe that it wasn't anything she'd said or done that had caused her to go. Of course, what she'd written wouldn't stop her mother worrying but there was nothing else she could have done, Christina reasoned, as the train began to gather speed, taking her further and further away from the source of her troubles.

Áine would know what to do, she told herself

again. She was the only one she could talk to about what had been going on these past weeks. She simply couldn't put up with them any longer. She just had to go.

The train hurtled on its way across the midlands. Christina had been to the west of Ireland only once before. She'd been about nine at the time and remembered staying with her parents in a comfortable, family-run hotel, within walking distance of a little place called Spiddal, a few miles outside Galway city. It had been called 'The Park' something or other. She racked her brain now to remember its full name, but couldn't. They'd been 'blessed with the weather' as the proprietor had told them several times, and almost every morning during their stay she and her mother and father had driven off to one or other of the many beautiful beaches further out in Connemara. Her favourite was Carraroe. It was a coral strand and, although it had been hard on her feet, she'd gladly forfeited the chance to make sandcastles and instead spent hours collecting different-shaped pieces of coral along the gleaming white shore. It was shortly after that holiday that her father had become ill and by the time summer came around again, he was dead. Once she said to her mother that she'd love to go back to Carraroe but her mother had shied away from the suggestion and Christina hadn't mentioned it again. Too many memories probably, Christina thought, as she turned to look out the window. She tried to concentrate on her book but exhaustion and the rocking of the train soon sent her off into an uneasy sleep.

'Ticket, please. Ticket please, Miss.'

Christina stared sleepily up at the man in the navy uniform, for a moment uncertain of where she was.

'Sorry to waken ya, love, but I have to do me job,' the ticket collector said cheerfully in a strong Dublin accent.

Christina reached into her anorak pocket, trying not to show how nervous she was.

'Travelling alone?' The man asked the dreaded question as he punched the ticket she handed him.

She nodded.

'Day off school, then?'

Again she nodded.

'Not a holyday, I hope,' he said with a hearty laugh. 'If it is, then I'm in big trouble with the Man above. No chance of Mass now.'

Despite herself, Christina managed a slight smile and, anxious to put any worry about Mass out of the poor man's head, said, 'No, no, it isn't a holyday. My grandmother's not too well and my class-teacher gave me the day off school to go over to visit her.' The ease with which the lies came out surprised her.

'Ah, that's the kind of teacher ya want, isn't it now, love? One with a bit of feelin'. Well, I hope ya won't find yer Granny too bad,' he said, moving over to the passenger on the other side of the carriage.

Immediately he turned away, Christina took up her book again and pretended to read. She could almost hear her heart thumping. She was well aware that a thirteen-year-old travelling unaccompanied during school term might cause people to ask questions. She'd managed to get through it this time, but she hoped she wouldn't have another such experience before the journey was over.

Not too long after the ticket collector had gone, Christina was glad to see a steward, pulling a tea-trolley behind him, come through the sliding door of her carriage. She'd been dying for something to drink and eat, but had been reluctant to leave her seat and walk down to the dining-car. She'd decided it would be best to stay where she was for the whole journey and remain as inconspicuous as possible in case there was someone who knew her travelling on the train.

When the trolley arrived she asked the steward for a carton of tea and a Club Milk. She'd already spent eleven of her mother's twenty pounds on her train ticket and she was conscious of the need to be as thrifty as possible with what she had left. Just as she handed over the money, the dividing door of the carriage slid open again, and out of the corner of her eye Christina caught sight of a dark-haired, olive-skinned girl. The carton in her hand began to shake, a few drops of the hot tea spilling over on to her anorak.

'All right, Miss?' the young steward enquired.

'Yes, I'm OK,' Christina assured him hastily, her face flushing.

For a moment she'd thought the girl was Siobhán. Christina knew she was being ridiculous but she couldn't help it, she just couldn't stop herself from trembling. When she'd seen the girl come through the door, she'd had the most awful sensation of being trapped, the feeling that, even though she'd travelled almost half-way across the country, Siobhán still had the power to appear out of nowhere, to taunt her as she tried to get away. She was more than ever convinced that she'd been right to set out on this journey. After the way she'd just reacted, she knew she had to get help soon.

She sat back in her seat and tried to relax, sipping her tea and eating the chocolate biscuit. The book lay open on her lap but she made no attempt to return to her reading, feeling all the time that every eye in the carriage was on her. Christina had lost all interest in looking at the countryside. She was willing the miles to pass, anxiously waiting for the journey to be over.

Chapter Seven

Her legs were stiff from sitting when the train finally pulled into Westport station. It was almost five o'clock when Christina stepped on to the platform, which was deserted except for the few people who'd got off the train. Her bag slung over her shoulder, she walked slowly towards the exit, giving the other passengers a wide berth. She stopped for a few minutes before a large poster on display near the exit gate. It read 'Westport House and Children's Zoo'. It showed the beautiful eighteenth-century home of Lord Altamont, which for a number of years now had been open to the public. She remembered Áine telling her all about a day she'd spent there with her family the previous summer. 'It was really brilliant, Christina,' she could almost hear Áine's voice say.

Turning, she made her way out of the station, then realised that it was getting dark already. She stood uncertainly, wondering which direction she should take. She knew it would be silly to ask anyone; the last thing she wanted to do was draw attention to herself. She walked a short distance and was relieved to see a signpost a little further on. She read the placenames. One arm was pointing to the Westport Heritage Centre, another indicating the direction of a place called Murrisk, yet another pointing the way to the county town of Mayo, Castlebar. None of these was of any help to Christina in deciding which way she should go, but the fourth name on the signpost stirred a vague feeling of recognition. Louisburgh, it read.

'Louisburgh,' Christina mused, as she read the name aloud. Louisburgh…yes, that's the way, she thought with relief, remembering Áine saying in one of her letters that the farm was off the Louisburgh road. She had asked Áine where the name had come from and Áine had replied to her in a letter that is had been founded by the Brown family in the eighteenth century and named after their daughter, Louisa.

She began walking as quickly as she could, conscious that it was getting darker by the minute. Soon she was outside the town, its lights growing dimmer with every step she took. For a moment she felt frightened. For the first time that day she realised exactly what she'd done—run away from home. No one else knew where she was or where she was heading. For a moment, she wondered if she had the courage to continue. She could turn around now and go back. But what good would that do? No, she'd come this far. Nothing was going to stop her seeing Áine now, nothing. Taking a deep breath, she began to walk resolutely on.

Soon, Christina found herself completely dependent on the moon to light her way. Once or twice a cloud floated across its face, blocking the light, and each time she prayed the night would stay clear, knowing that without the help of the moon she'd never find the place she was looking for. Very few cars passed, but as soon as she saw oncoming lights Christina quickly ducked down into the grass verge at the side of the road until the car had gone by, hoping the driver hadn't seen her.

On one occasion she wasn't quick enough and the headlights of a car picked her out as she scrambled for cover. A few yards further on, the car screeched to a stop and the door was thrown open. Christina didn't move but she could hear the driver stepping out, and a rough voice saying, 'Ye may as well show yerself. I know ye're there.'

Christina got up from her knees, brushing off some of the muck and grass that clung to her jeans.

'What the hell are ye doing, walking half-way out in the middle of the road? D'ye want to be killed?'

The bulky figure of a man came towards her and as he reached her he brought his face up close to hers in an effort to see her in the dark. Christina took a step back, but wasn't quick enough.

'Ah, a young one, is it?' the man said, grabbing hold of her arm. 'And a good-lookin' one at that,' he added, pulling her nearer to him.

'Leave me alone, let go of me,' Christina said, struggling to free herself.

'Particular, are ye?' the man sneered, still holding her firmly with one hand, his other one cupping her chin as he pulled her in even closer to him. His hand was rough and hard, and as his thumb and forefinger dug into the two sides of her cheek, her skin began to throb under their pressure. The darkness and the peaked cap he wore well down over his forehead prevented Christina from seeing his face properly but the smell of his breath made her recoil, and she knew he'd been drinking. He began mumbling obscenities and started tugging at the zip of her anorak, cursing loudly as it stuck half-way. Realising the danger she was in, Christina lowered her head and sank her teeth sharply into his hand, at the same time giving him the hardest possible kick on the shin with a strength she didn't know she possessed.

'Ye little bitch,' the man cursed angrily, taken by surprise. As he slackened his hold, she kicked him again, finally managing to wrench herself free. Then she raced for her life, away into the surrounding darkness. She heard him curse again as he fumbled his way back towards the car, and then shortly afterwards, as she huddled down behind a clump of trees, she listened as he tried to start the engine once or twice before eventually succeeding. Gears crunched as he finally pulled away, Christina held her breath until the car passed the spot where she was hiding. Clenching her fist, she put it to her lips, biting down hard upon it in an effort to stifle her sobs as she realised what a narrow escape she'd had. Was anything worth all this, she wondered, as she crouched there in the dark field. She'd never have come in contact with that awful man, never have had to run away, if it hadn't been for Siobhán and Helen. How she hated the pair of them.

Wearily she got to her feet and made her way back on to the road. It was only then that she remembered her bag. In her frantic rush to get away from that man, she'd forgotten all about it. It must be lying somewhere back there in the ditch. Slowly she headed back down the road, trying to judge the spot where the car had stopped. She knew there must be skid-marks, but at this time of night there was no possibility of making them out. After searching about in the dark as best she could, she gave up and continued on her solitary journey.

The November evening was growing colder now. Christina pulled the hood of her anorak tightly around her head and pushed her hands deep into its pockets. Her feet were beginning to feel the cold, too, and in an effort to keep them warm she brought her Doc Martens down heavily with each step she took.

As she walked, her eyes searched constantly for something that might point her in the direction of the O'Neills' farm, or at least confirm that she was on the right road. When she'd covered what she judged to be three, or maybe four miles, she reached a crossroads. Again, she studied the signpost before her, relieved to find that she was still heading in the right direction. A quarter of an hour later Christina saw an outline against the dark sky. At first it looked to her like the silhouette of a big, old house, but as she drew nearer she saw that it was, in fact, a ruin. Her heart began to beat more quickly. Even though she'd never seen it, she had a strong hunch that this was the remains of the old castle Áine had told her about. She'd said the farm was a few miles from Westport and that the ruins of an old castle were close by. Well, she must now be about the right distance from the town, and these were the only ruins she'd happened upon so far. A bit further on, there was a turning off the main road into a side road. She presumed that it led up to the ruins and made her way towards it. After walking a little way up, she found that it tapered off into a narrow boreen. Through some tall trees ahead of her she could make out the lights of a house, and not too far to the right of these she could see another much bigger cluster of lights which she decided had to be the village of Castledonagh.

Christina found a gap in the hedge and, squeezing through, crossed the field towards the remains of the old castle. She climbed through a crumbling gap in its walls and dropped down inside. The walls were extremely thick, making the interior surprisingly small. Most of the upper floor had collapsed, but one corner held firm and she headed over to it, searching for the most sheltered spot. She stumbled a few times in the dark before she finally found the best place, and, making herself as comfortable as she could on the hard uneven earth, she settled down, resting her head against the cold, damp stone wall.

She knew there was no chance of seeing Áine tonight unless, of course, she went up and knocked on the farmhouse door. But then Áine's parents would immediately telephone her mother and she'd be sent home and back to school. And school meant Siobhán and Helen! That was something that mustn't happen. She had to speak to Áine first, and alone.

She accepted the fact that she'd have to spend the night in the castle, cold and damp as it was, although she shivered at the thought. She'd wait and watch out for her friend in the morning. If she was at the right place, that is...But this must surely be the boreen where Áine caught the school bus each day. It had to be, Christina told herself fiercely.

Chapter Eight

Impossible as it seemed, Christina must have slept. For what must have been hours she had simply sat staring into the darkness. Her eyes ached, but she'd managed to keep them open. But in the end sleep must have overcome her, for now the luminous dial of her watch told her that it was almost ten to seven. The November sky was still as dark as night.

She got up from her cramped position and began pacing up and down trying to get the pins-and-needles out of her legs and at the same time hoping to warm herself a little. She reached into her coat pocket, found the last two squares of a bar of chocolate and ate them hungrily. It was stupid not bringing something to eat, she chided herself, relishing the last few flakes of chocolate on her tongue. She thought of all the sweet- and cake-shops she'd walked past in Dublin the day before. Why hadn't she thought of buying something for the journey? The last food she'd eaten was the previous mid-afternoon on the train and then it was only a cup of tea and a Club Milk. Yet she'd gone into Chapters and bought a book, making sure she'd have something to read. Now she didn't have the book, either. It had been in her bag and, thanks to that revolting man from the night before, she hadn't even got that! She could have done with her school jumper now, too, to slip on under her anorak for some extra warmth, and her gaberdine boat would have come in very handy.

She positioned herself at a spot in the wall where a huge piece of masonry had long ago crumbled and fallen away, a perfect vantage point to observe the boreen. For the next hour she didn't take her weary eyes off it. At last, she thought she heard the sound of voices and, taking a chance, she left her hiding place and scurried across the open field until she reached the cover of the hedge. She'd been right; she could hear someone talking. Crouching for extra cover, she waited as the voices drew nearer, and as they grew more distinct she recognised Thomas's, and, then, to her delight, Áine's.

Her delight quickly faded. Áine wasn't alone; she was with the twins! Why hadn't she thought of that? Of course she'd be with Karen and Thomas. Didn't they all travel on the same bus? She couldn't risk approaching Áine while her brother and sister were with her, and take the chance that they would reveal the fact that she was here in Castledonagh. She bit back a sob as she saw the three familiar figures come into view in the still dusky mornhng. They looked so happy, talking and laughing together. Then Thomas shouldered his way between the two girls in a rush to be first down to the bus pick-up point. They passed within a few feet of where she was hiding, Áine's red hair blowing in wisps around her face, as though determined to escape from under the snug hat she wore. Christina had to bite her lip to stop herself calling out to her. But as she was giving up all hope of making contact, she heard Áine grumble loudly, 'Oh drat! I've left my history book on the kitchen table and we've got an hour class today.'

Christina held her breath.

'Look,' Áine said to Thomas and Karen, 'better go on ahead, you two. I'll run back and get it. Tell

Johnny I won't be long and see if he'll wait a minute. Try not to let him go without me, will you?' she urged, before turning quickly to head back up towards the house.

'OK,' her brother replied, 'but hurry, Áine. You know what Johnny's like if he has to wait.'

As the other two moved out of earshot, and Áine headed back up the boreen, Christina called her name in a low voice.

She saw the other girl stop, startled, and look around uncertainly in all directions, trying to find where the voice was coming from.

'Áine, over here, over here,' Christina hissed urgently and stood up, her dark head showing just above the top of the hedge.

'Christina!' Áine gaped at her, her blue eyes wide and unbelieving, all thoughts of her history book forgotten.

'Ssh, shh,' Christina warned, pointing in the direction of the twins, and then motioned to her to come through to her side of the hedge.

'I can't believe I'm seeing properly,' Áine said as she squeezed through. 'What on earth are you doing here? And at this hour of the morning. Christina, where did you come from?'

She quickly took in her friend's damp clothes and generally dishevelled look. 'Something's wrong, Chris. Tell me what it is. You look terrible.' She touched Christina's face as she spoke, brushing a piece of grime from her cheek.

'Oh, Áine,' Christina began, unable to hold back her tears at the look of concern on her friend's face. 'Áine, I don't know where to begin. Everything's gone wrong since you left, everything…'

She was interrupted in mid-sentence by the blaring sound of a horn. The school bus had arrived.

'Oh no,' Áine exclaimed, 'it's here already. Look, Christina, go on up to the house. I know something's wrong, but Mammy'll look after you until I get home from school. You can tell me everything then. I must go now or I'll be late.'

'No, no, I can't do that. I've got to stay here,' Christina said, panic in her voice.

'But why?' Áine asked. 'Why can't you?'

'It'd take too long to explain now. Go on, run or you'll miss the bus. Watch for me on the way home,' she pleaded. Before Áine could answer Christina had started back across the field to the shelter of the ruins.

Áine stood uncertainly for a moment, looking after her, and then, as Johnny once again sounded the horn impatiently, she began to run down the boreen.

All during school, Áine thought of nothing else but Christina's unexpected arrival. Appearing like that out of nowhere! Something must be terribly wrong but she hadn't a clue what it could be. All Christina's letters had sounded so normal; there was no hint in them of her having any problems. Áine regretted more and more that she'd left her so quickly. She should have let the stupid bus go and stayed and made her go up to the house with her. Missing one day of school wouldn't have been the end of the world. But she'd been taken so much by surprise that she couldn't think straight. She'd been looking forward to seeing Christina as soon as they could both arrange it, but she'd never imagined it would happen like this. And it was so completely out of character for her friend. She was a gentle girl who never caused any trouble at home or in school, and yet here she was miles away from Dublin, right in the middle of the school term! Áine found it hard to take in.

She wondered then how long Christina had been waiting there before she'd arrived. The first train from Dublin wouldn't get her into Westport until midday—she knew that from years of visits to this part of the country. So it was probable that Christina had travelled down the day before. Surely she hadn't spent the night in the ruins in this terribly cold November weather. She could catch pneumonia after a night out in weather like that, Áine thought, or, worse still, she could have died from exposure.

As the day dragged on, Áine was torn with indecision.

Should she go against her friend's request and ring her mother at the farm and tell her what had happened? Maybe ask her to go down to McDonagh's Castle and look for Christina? For some reason Áine didn't yet understand, she knew that Christina wanted to talk to her first about whatever was wrong. So, she did nothing, just got more and more worried about her as the day progressed.

Only eleven o'clock.

For Christina, too, the day dragged. The morning seemed endless and she found herself looking at her watch, willing the hands to move faster. Still almost five hours to go before Áine would be returning from school, she told herself resignedly, as she swung her arms and stamped her feet in an attempt to keep warm. The day was still bitterly cold, and the chill November air seemed to seep deeper and deeper into her bones with each minute that passed. Her stomach ached for something to eat and her throat felt raw. In her troubled, anxious state, Christina found the stillness of the countryside unnerving. The silence was broken only occasionally by the harsh call of a crow, or the muffled bellow of an animal in a far-off field.

Her thoughts turned to her mother. How did she react when she read the note? Had she realised that money was missing from her purse? Had she called the gardai? Was there anyone with her right now? All these questions flew around inside her brain as the minutes ticked slowly by. Finding the thought of her mother too upsetting, she tried to push it to the back of her mind, as in an attempt to occupy herself and pass the time, she began counting the huge, centuries-old stone slabs in the wall opposite.

Eventually she stopped looking at her watch, instead trying to judge what time it was by the amount of light in the sky. At one stage in the early afternoon, she risked going a little nearer to the main road to see if there was any sign of the bus coming. It was far too early but at least it broke the monotony. There was nothing to see but a ramshackle lorry trundling by.

Then, just when she thought it was never going to arrive, Christina heard the faint noise of the bus's wheels crunching to a stop, and soon afterwards the sound of voices reached her for the second time that day. This time she didn't leave her hiding place, but stayed still, watching. Thomas and Karen went running past and a moment or two later she heard Áine's voice softly humming a song they'd both learned in the school choir just before she'd left St Mary's. Trust Áine, she thought, the ghost of a smile crossing her face.

Within seconds she saw her friend hurrying across the field and in no time the red-haired girl had climbed through the opening in the wall and landed beside her. The two girls threw their arms around one another in a fierce hug, both talking at once. Finally, both realising that neither of them could grasp one word of what the other was saying, they suddenly became quiet, and then, looking each other in the face, they burst into a fit of giggles. It was a strange sensation for Christina, who hadn't laughed properly for weeks and, becoming almost hysterical, she found it difficult to stop.

'Now then,' said Áine, serious at last. She took Christina by the arm. 'Tell me what this is all about.'

In a rush, her voice shaking, Christina told her all that had happened in the weeks since she left.

'I can't believe it. You poor thing. How could they be so cruel?' Áine was torn beteween sympathy for Christina and fury at the bullies. 'That miserable, twisted, sneering pair of...' She broke off. 'But no matter what, you should have told your mother or confided in Mrs Kenny. Any of the teachers would have been glad to help, you know that, Chris.'

'I know, but, you see...'

'No "buts".' That's exactly what we're going to

do,' Áine reassured her.

'But you don't know what those two are like, what they'll do to me if I talk,' Christina cried. 'I thought there'd be some other way, that you could tell me what to do, or what to say to them so that I could handle it myself. I don't want my mother involved...and...I'm not sure Mrs Kenny would believe me, anyway.'

'Believe you? Why wouldn't she? Of course she will,' Áine said confidently. 'Now look, come on up to the house with me. You're shivering and, from what I can see, you've caught a fine cold. Your mother must be going mad worrying about you. We'll ring her the minute we get in.'

Christina looked at her in horror.

'But Áine, you don't understand. Just tell me what to say to them to make them stop, to make them leave me alone. Please, Áine,' she begged. 'You'd know what to do if it were you they were bullying, wouldn't you? I just want to know what to do,' she repeated despairingly.

'Chris,' Áine said patiently. 'I've told you, you've got to confide in your mother or someone in authority at school. Call their bluff. Do exactly what they don't want you to do—tell. That's what *I'd* do.'

But no matter how much Áine pleaded with her, Christina, now completely distraught, wouldn't agree to go up to the house with her and Áine was at a loss to know what to do. Realising the state her friend was in, she could see it was no use trying to reason with her any longer. Whatever it was that Siobhán and Helen had plotted to do to her couldn't have been worse than this, Áine thought, as she looked at Christina, now sitting huddled in the corner, her knees tucked up under her chin, a glazed look in her eyes, muttering, 'No use, no use…'

Bending down beside her, Áine put her arm around her friend and said gently, 'Don't worry, Christina. We'll sort it out, we will. Everything will be all right, I promise. Just sit there now. Don't move and I'll be back in a minute.'

She looked back at her just before climbing through the gap in the wall and saw that she hadn't moved, her cold pinched face still wearing the same trance-like expression. Deciding she'd better get help as quickly as possible, Áine jumped down on to the ground outside. Her hat blew off as she encountered a sudden gust of wind but she raced across the field, her red hair blowing wildly. She slipped through the opening in the hedge and ran on and on up the boreen until she reached the house. Bursting through the back door she shouted, 'Mammy, Mammy,' breathlessly, at the top of her voice.

Áine's mother was standing in the huge kitchen of Woodville, kneading a large round of dough, when the telephone rang.

Why was it, she wondered with a sigh, that whenever she had her hands in a basin of sudsy water, or was up to her eyes in flour, the phone had to ring. Solid as the walls of the house were, she could just about hear the twins having their usual struggle as they changed out of their school uniforms. No use calling that pair, she knew. By the time she'd make herself heard above the noise they were making, the caller would have hung up. She glanced across the kitchen to where her mother-in-law had dozed off in the armchair. Both men of the house were out working on the farm, so there was nothing else for it but to give her hands a quick rub in her apron and answer it herself.

She was surprised but delighted to find it was Christina's mother on the line, and greeted her warmly. But as she listened to the distraught voice, her smile quickly faded and a frown creased her forehead.

'My God, Angela, that's terrible news, terrible,' she said incredulously.

'I knew you'd telephone if she did contact you,' Angela Miles was saying, 'but I just had to ring anyway, just in case. You know, with she and Áine being so close, I thought that maybe…'

'Of course, I understand. But no, we haven't heard anything from her here.'

Christina's mother began to say something else, but their conversation was suddenly interrupted by someone calling loudly.

'Sorry, Angela, I didn't catch what you said that time. I think someone's calling me,' Maureen O'Neill said, putting her hand over the receiver. Turning, she put her finger to her lips in an effort to quieten her elder daughter who'd just rushed shouting into the room.

It took Áine less than twenty minutes to reach the house and return with her mother to where she'd left Christina. She called her friend's name as they approached, expecting to see her emerge from her hiding place, but there was no response to her call. When she and her mother climbed inside the now dusky enclosure, to their dismay they found there was no trace of her whatsoever.

After Áine had gone, Christina sat where she was for a short time, the silence hanging heavily over her. Her throat burned, her stomach felt as though it were full of cold air, her clothes were damp and she was shivering uncontrollably. The terrible realisation that her journey to Mayo had all been for nothing was beginning to take hold.

Áine couldn't help her; she could only tell her what she should have done in the first place. She had been her only hope. If *she* couldn't help, then who could? She gave a little whimper as she dragged herself to her feet. There was no use staying here any longer. There was no solution to her problem to be found in this freezing, windswept spot.

Climbing through the opening, she stumbled out to the field and, slightly disorientated now, began heading further out into the open countryside. She increased her pace, not caring which direction she took. Every so often now a harsh cough racked her and a sharp pain shot through her chest, but still she hurried on.

Chapter Nine

Torches and storm lamps dotted the night as they searched for Christina. As soon as Áine and her mother had discovered that she was gone, they telephoned the gardai, who were quickly on the scene. The local branch of the Civil Defence was also called out and together they combed every inch of the ruins, the surrounding farms and outhouses. Still there was no sign of her. The gardai had also checked Westport Station, in case Christina had taken it into her head to return home, but neither the ticket-seller nor the stationmaster had seen anyone fitting her description boarding the Dublin train that evening.

As news of the young girl's disappearance spread through the village, many people from the surrounding area began arriving at Woodville, offering their services, anxious to help in any small way they could. Group after group of searchers set off and as the number of volunteers began to grow, they started to fan out, covering a much wider area. The night was clear but again bitterly cold, and fears for Christina grew with each hour that passed. The local doctor had been called and had questioned Áine at length about Christina's physical and mental state. When she told him that Christina already seemed to have developed a chill from spending the previous night in the open, and that she'd been extremely distressed and perhaps even confused towards the end of their conversation, he shook his head, leaving them in no doubt as to how serious the situation was.

After midnight, red-eyed and weary, Áine still

plodded along beside her father. So far she'd resisted all his efforts to persuade her to go home and rest but he knew she was exhausted and unable to take much more. Once again he suggested she get some rest.

'But Daddy, Christina came here to see me. If I'd been able to help her this wouldn't have happened.'

'Now don't blame yourself, Áine,' he said gently, reflecting that the poor child must have been in a bad way to head off to spend another night in conditions like this when the warmth and comfort of Woodville had been only minutes away. 'It's not because of anything you did or didn't do that this has happened. It's what those others did to her that's the cause of it all.' But he knew he was wasting his time trying to convince his daughter that she wasn't responsible in any way for her friend's disappearance.

The search-party was now heading in the direction of Locan Wood. To Áine it seemed like a place she'd never set eyes on before. They'd always spent time in the wood when they came to Mayo on holidays and the first Sunday after they arrived at Woodville this autumn the whole family had gone walking in it. That day, the September sunshine had shone through the trees but now, as it loomed up dark and forbidding before them, it was as unfamiliar and eerie to Áine as the dark side of the moon.

Jim O'Neill put his arm around his daughter's shoulders, pulling her closer to him. Things would start looking bad for Christina unless they found her soon, he thought, as they reached the first range of trees. But he said nothing, not wanting to upset his daughter any further. The searchers began moving in through the trees, torches flashing in every direction, all the time calling Christina's name. But the only sounds in the night were the twigs that snapped beneath their feet, the occasional lonely hoot of an owl and the swish of the ferns as they moved through them.

The search was finally called off in the early hours of the morning. It was a very worried and weary group which arrived back at the farmhouse. The twins were in bed, despite all their pleas to their mother to let them stay up until the search party returned. She had decided that they'd be better off at school the next day, out of the way of all that was going on, and that they needed their sleep. But Áine's grandapents were in the kitchen, helping to serve the very welcome hot soup and sandwiches. When they had all thawed out a bit, the local sergeant called for everyone's attention, requesting volunteers for a renewed search the following morning. The numbers would be smaller because most people had to go to work but it was agreed that the wood should be combed again, just in case they'd missed Christina. The ferns were very dense in places, the sergeant pointed out, and if she'd fallen asleep from exhaustion, it was just possible that she hadn't heard their calls. There was a general murmur of agreement throughout the kitchen.

Sitting silently among the adults, Áine couldn't help thinking about the lake a little beyond Locan Wood. No one had mentioned it yet, but she knew it was on everyone's mind. If Christina had managed to make her way through the wood, then a little further on she was bound to come upon the lake. She didn't know the area, and in the dark of night, anything could have happened. Áine felt her throat tighten at the thought. She couldn't bear to think about it any longer. Tiredness overcame her and she said goodnight to her parents before leaving the kitchen. But from the hall she heard the sergeant saying, 'You know, lads, we'll have to have a look down at the lake, too, as soon as it's bright. I didn't want to mention it while young Áine was here—she's upset enough as it is—but it's just possible her friend may have headed in that direction.'

Again there was a murmur of agreement as he continued. 'We'll get a few lads from the sub-aqua club to come with us. There was no point in asking them to come tonight; sure they'd never see a thing in the dark.'

Áine couldn't listen to any more and hurried up the stairs to her room, biting back the tears. She threw herself down on the bed and cried and cried. Poor Christina. Where was she now? Her best friend—how could this be happening to her? It was like something you'd read in a book, something that happened to other people but couldn't happen to them.

'Dear God, let her be safe,' she prayed, clenching her hands together. 'Don't let her be in the lake. Let her be alive, please let her be alive.'

Early the next morning, Christina's bag was found. A young boy cycling to school had seen it thrown in the ditch. He took it to school with him and showed it to his teacher. When she saw that it had a girl's school uniform inside, she remembered the news of the missing teenager and went directly to the garda barracks with it The sergeant phoned Woodville and informed Áine's father of the latest development. Áine and her mother stood apprehensively beside him.

'Well, any news?' Maureen O'Neill asked as soon as he hung up.

'Yes, some…but nothing conclusive,' he answered, fingering his neat brown beard, his expression conveying to her that the news wasn't good.

'Tell us, Daddy, what did he say?' Áine implored.

'They've found her bag. A young fellow on his way to school found it sticking out of a ditch, a good bit along the Westport road. Her school uniform was in it.'

'She must have been heading back there to catch the train to Dublin,' Áine's mother decided. 'If she didn't go to the station, then where did she go?'

'There's something else…' Jim O'Neill paused, looking at his daughter's face, wishing he didn't have to tell her what it was.

'What is it, Daddy?'

'I'm afraid there were tyre skid-marks near where the bag was found. The sergeant and one of his men went to the spot and noticed that there were signs of a scuffle in the area around the ditch…'

'Oh my God, they don't think someone attacked her, or pulled her into a car, or something, do they?' Áine's mother asked anxiously, Noticing the sudden pallor of her daughter's face, she immediately regretted the question.

'Well, you know the gardai, they don't say much until they're sure.'

'Are they certain it was Christina's bag?' Áine

asked. 'It might belong to someone else. I don't remember seeing her with one yesterday.'

'I'm sorry, love, but it's Christina's all right. The sergeant said they found a book in it with her name written inside the cover.'

A look of fear crossed his daughter's face, and she covered her eyes with her hands for a moment as though trying to block out some horrible picture. Her voice was slightly muffled as she asked, 'Oh, Dad, you know what Mammy just said about...maybe someone dragging her into a car. You don't think...?' Áine didn't finish.

Jim O'Neill took his daughter gently by the hand and led her over to a chair. 'Come on, Áine, sit down here now for a minute and try not to be so upset. There's no point in thinking anything just yet. We'll just have to keep hoping for the best. Christina will be OK. I'm sure she will. Right now it probably looks much worse than it actually is.'

Christina's mother arrived at lunchtime. She'd travelled on the morning train from Dublin which got her into Westport just after midday. Áine's father collected her from the station and immediately took her out to the farm. As they travelled the same road that her daughter had travelled two nights before, Angela Miles gazed out the window of the car and wondered, yet again, if all this could be really happening.

When she had found Christina's note, at first she couldn't believe it. But when she'd phoned the school and found Christina hadn't come in that morning, she'd been absolutely frantic with worry. After ringing around all her friends at Mr Doyle's suggestion and coming up with nothing, she'd finally called the gardai. In the confusion, she hadn't even thought of mentioning the O'Neills to them, never dreaming that Christina would have travelled all the way to Westport. It was an amazing coincidence that she'd been on the phone to Maureen O'Neill the next day when Áine had come running in the door with the news that she'd actually spoken to her missing daughter.

During the drive from the station, Jim O'Neill filled her in on all that had taken place so far. He dropped her at the door of Woodville and went off again to join the search. Angela Miles stepped out of the car at the front of the house, holding a small overnight bag, the collar of her sheepskin coat pulled up around her neck, huge dark smudges under her eyes. 'Angela,' Maureen O'Neill said gently, coming to the door to meet her.

In the kitchen she settled her in a comfortable armchair close to the range and handed her a cup of tea. 'There you are now, Angela, drink it up while it's hot. Are you sure you won't even have a sandwich or a biscuit with it? I know you must be sick with worry, but try to relax a bit.'

'But this latest news...' Christina's mother began, thinking of what Áine's father had told her about the car and the sign of a struggle.

'I know, I know, but please God it'll mean nothing. I'm sure it won't be long now before they find her.' Maureen O'Neill hoped that she sounded more confident than she felt.

The search party had been out since dawn, but when the news came from the gardai about the discovery of Christina's bag, the searchers decided that it would be more beneficial to split up, one half heading to the area where her bag had been found to search the ditch and surrounding fields, while the other half continued to search Locan Wood once more, as decided the night before.

So far there was no word from either group. Áine had wanted to go out with them again, but this time her father insisted she stay at home. If they didn't find Christina in the wood or somewhere near the spot on the road where the car had pulled in, he knew the next place to be searched would be the lake. If the result of that search had a tragic outcome, neither he nor his wife wanted their daughter to witness it. Áine came into the kitchen now, her usual lively face tired and drawn, and going over to Christina's mother, put her arms around her. For a moment or two they clung to each other without speaking. Then Angela Miles questioned Áine about what Christina had told her, wanting to know every detail of what Siobhán and Helen had done to her daughter. 'Did she ever mention anything in her letters to you about all this bullying, about how badly those two girls were treating her?' she asked, her voice trembling as she tried to keep from breaking down.

'No, never. Not a word,' Áine said. 'She kept it all to herself until she came here.'

'My poor child. If only I'd paid more attention,' Christina's mother whispered, 'especially that day I noticed her a bit off form. If only, if only...'

There was silence in the large old kitchen, as the three of them sat there feeling helpless, a silence broken only by the gentle hissing of the logs as they burnt inside the range.

Chapter Ten

Gloom hung over St Mary's.

In the staffroom the teachers were subdued as they discussed the situation and waited anxiously for news of Christina's whereabouts. The two most affected by what had happened were Mrs Kenny and Mr Doyle.

'Her poor mother must be in a terrible state,' the headmaster said to Mrs Kenny as they had a cup of tea during break. 'I can't imagine what would have made the poor child do something so drastic. Did you notice anything that the rest of us might have missed, being her year-head?'

It was a few minutes before Mrs Kenny spoke. 'You know, I did notice a deterioration in her work just before half-term. I blame myself for not enquiring more into the reason for it,' she said. 'Whatever was bothering her must have had a terrible effect on her to make her run off like this. I got the feeling once that she was a bit lonely with her mother still out at work every day when she arrived home, but there must be more to it than that.'

'Her mother said the O'Neills seemed to think it had something to do with school all right, but of course it was all very confused and they didn't want to say any more over the phone. She's been gone over twenty-four hours now. The longer it goes on the less hopeful I am,' Mr Doyle said, shaking his head.

He'd called a general assembly that morning in the school hall. There was a tense silence as the girls digested the news of Christina's disappearance, quickly followed by low murmers of excited comment. The headmaster asked that any girl who had even the slightest notion as to why Christina had gone should come forward. He told them that it was possible that some problem at school might have caused her to run away but he couldn't be in any way specific as to what it might have been. However, he stressed, even the smallest piece of information might assist the gardai in the search for her.

So far, none of the girls had come forward with anything which might help.

All the teachers who had contact with Christina examined their conscience to discover where they'd gone so wrong in their relationship with her that the poor girl hadn't been able to approach any of them with her problems. It was terrible to think that she might have wanted to talk to one of them about what was bothering her, and for some reason just couldn't bring herself to do it.

In the corridors of St Mary's, Christina's name was whispered, as girls went into huddles to discuss what had happened. Rumours were rife about why she'd gone. Some girls were saying her mother had always been far too strict with her and that she'd finally grown tired of it. Others said she'd simply run away for a dare. But a third rumour was that she'd been caught taking money from the school shop, a rumour that Siobhán had latched on to immediately and was now taking great pleasure in spreading as widely as possible. She stood now, in the centre of a large group, discussing it excitedly. Strangely, for once Helen wasn't beside her. She was standing right at the back of the circle of girls, looking even paler than usual, her hand rubbing a long red weal which ran the full length of her left cheek. She didn't join in the conversation, but stood there on the fringes, never once taking her eyes from Siobhán's animated face

No doubt there would be other rumours as the day went on; the two girls who knew the truth were saying nothing.

Once again the search of Locan Wood had proved fruitless. Word had also come through from the gardai at Westport that there was nothing found in the search of the roadside ditch and surrounding fields. Christina's mother didn't know whether to feel hopeful or not. Feelings of intense anxiety alternated with anger at the two girls who had made her daughter's life a misery and driven her to this.

As the evening began to draw in, attention was firmly focused on the lake, which was about half a mile beyond Locan Wood. It was a popular spot for family outings at weekends, or during the long summer school holidays. If the day were particularly good, there were boats for hire for a trip to one of the small islands nestling in the middle. Around the edge were numerous small shingle inlets, appearing like perfect spots for bathing. But it was a treacherous lake, the water deepening suddenly in places only a few feet from the edge.

On this bleak November day, the lake wasn't in the least inviting, its smooth surface looking like a huge dull grey mirror. Even at the lakeshore, there was hardly any movement in the water, not even the usual gentle lapping.

At the water's edge, John Joe Moriarty, a weather-beaten little man, stood talking loudly to the sergeant, gesticulating as he spoke.

'Sure, I'm tellin' ye, I tied it up at the usual spot yesterday evenin' and now it's gone,' John Joe said, his face flushed with excitement.

'In God's name, man, why didn't ye tell us before now?' the sergeant asked in exasperation, taking off his cap and scratching his balding head.

'An' how could I, will ye tell me that?' John Joe demanded angrily. 'Didn't I only discover it was gone meself half an hour ago when I came down to go out in it. An' it took me since then to traipse around the shore lookin' for the lot of ye.'

'Jim, over here,' the sergeant called, beckoning Áine's father over from where he stood talking to one of the sub-aqua divers. 'It seems that John Joe's boat has disappeared', the sergeant explained. 'He says he left it in its usual spot beside the lake yesterday evening and now it's gone. There wasn't a sign of it when he came down to go out in it an hour or so ago.'

'What do you think?' Jim O'Neill asked.

'Well now, it may have no connection whatever with the girl's disappearance, but we'd better get that motor launch started and see if we can find his boat out there anywhere.'

The sergeant, Áine's father and the diver, who was called Éamon, climbed into the launch. Within seconds the roar of its engine filled the still air, and they headed off. Slowly they circled the perimeter of the lake, eyes scanning every inch of it for a sign of John Joe's boat, but there was none. Disappointed, they revved the engine a little to increase their speed, and headed the launch out towards the middle. They circled each island, but again they were out of luck; there was still no sign of the missing boat. Dejected, they headed for shore.

Áine and Christina's mother were standing by the water's edge when the launch pulled in. They had got word of the missing boat at Woodville. They watched as Jim O'Neill and his companions climbed wearily out of the boat. Their anxious expressions asked a thousand questions. Putting his arms around both of them, Áine's father shook his head. 'Nothing, I'm afraid. There wasn't a sign of anything.'

Angela Miles began to sob softly. In an effort to comfort her, Jim O'Neill suggested, 'Look, it's beginning to get dark, but if the others are agreeable, we'll go out one more time.'

Christina's mother looked at him gratefully. In all the years she'd known the O'Neills, she'd never really appreciated just what good friends they were. Jim and Maureen and Jim's elderly parents had thrown their home open to her since her arrival, and no one could have been kinder. She had some idea now just how fond Christina had been of Áine. If she were half as good as her parents, she was a friend no one would want to lose. Poor Christina, she thought, how lonely she must have been without her.

Áine turned to her father. 'Let me go with you, Dad, please. I've just got this feeling that if I go…'

'No, Áine. You know how I feel about you being involved in all of this.'

'Oh, Dad, please, please. Just let me go this one time. I know it sounds crazy, but I feel as if she's out there somewhere calling to me.'

Jim O'Neill glanced uncertainly from one tearful face to the other. Angela Miles looked at him imploringly, as if she were convinced that Áine was right, and that by some sixth sense she might be able to help them find her daughter. He relented. 'OK then, let's go. But Angela, I think you should wait up at the house. We'll send up for you if we find anything. I'm sure the garda driver will give you a lift back.'

Once again the motor launch's engine swung into life. The four passengers circled the lake for the second time that afternoon, again without success, and headed for the islands. It was almost dusk now, the grey sky and the water beginning to merge into one. A train went by, its lonely whistle filling the evening air, the lights in its half-empty carriages sending out a warm glow for a moment or two as it passed.

Áine stood, stiffly at the front of the boat, her eyes searching in every direction, praying that she'd spot something. As the boat drew near the islands, the sergeant slowed down the motor, in order to get as close as possible to the rocky shores. One island in particular, the largest, had several big rocks jutting out from its northern end.

As they were passing this northern point, something caught Áine's eye.

'Wait,' she shouted over the roar of the engine. 'Wait. I'm sure I saw something over there,' she said excitedly. They edged the boat a little nearer to the rocks, trying to distinguish a shape in the dusk. After a few moments, Éamon pointed in the direction she'd indicated.

'She's right,' he said, 'there is something there, something wedged in between those two rocks. By now Áine's father and the sergeant could also just make out a dark shape.

'I'm almost certain it's a boat,' Éamon said. 'But we'll never be able to get the boat close enough to it from here. Try to find a safer place to land somewhere further up and in the meantime I'll swim over and have a look.' He hauled himself over the side into the freezing water and began swimming strongly towards the rocks.

It took the others several precious minutes to find a suitable place to berth the launch. They climbed quickly out and Áine began to run ahead, anxious to get back to where Éamon was. With darkness falling quickly, even in the few minutes they'd been separated from him, it had become more difficult to make out exactly where he'd come ashore. But soon Áine heard him calling, 'Here, I'm here. Quickly, I've found her.' She headed in the direction of his voice. Not knowing what to expect, her heart thundering in her chest, Áine ran faster than she'd ever run in her life, followed by her father and the sergeant.

They found Éamon bending down between the two rocks. Squeezing in beside him, Áine saw John Joe Moriarty's boat, wedged tightly. At one end, curled up in the bottom, was Christina. She was neither awake nor asleep, her breathing was shallow and rasping, her dark hair wet and clinging to her face. Áine leaned in and, touching her cheek, found it was icy cold. She gave a tiny, shocked whimper. Her father gently drew her aside as the men lifted

Christina and carried her carefully along the shore towards the motor launch.

When they got back on land, the sergeant radioed for an ambulance. A number of locals had gathered and, now, at Jim O'Neill's request, one of them ran up to the house to fetch Christina's mother. On the back seat of the garda car, Christina lay wrapped in a blanket, her eyes closed, her face deathly pale, not making the slightest move. Although the ambulance wasn't very long in coming, Áine found the wait interminable. She stood close to Christina's mother as it bumped its way down to the water's edge, blue light flashing, siren blaring. As the ambulance men placed Christina on a stretcher and lifted her into the vehicle, Angela Miles turned to Áine and gave her a kiss on the cheek. 'Go home now,' she said, 'and get something hot to drink. You've done all you can for the moment. I'll ring you from the hospital as soon as the doctor tells me anything.'

For just a few minutes during the trip to the County Hospital, Christina became lucid and, recognising her mother, smiled wanly. From her mumbled replies to her mother's gentle questions, it appeared that she didn't remember very clearly what had happened after Áine had left her the previous afternoon. She had somehow made her way to Locan Wood and then on towards the lake. When she came upon the boat, she'd been so cold and exhausted that instinct had led her to climb inside it for what little shelter it could offer. She thought she must have eventually fallen asleep, because the next thing she knew she felt a gentle rocking and, to her horror, she found herself adrift on the pitch-black water. She wasn't sure if she'd tried to get back to the shore or not—her memory becoming quite confused at this stage—but it wouldn't have made any difference anyway, because as her mother had heard, there had been no oars in the boat when they found it. It seemed that John Joe Moriarity was a cautious man and never left them in it. She did remember lying in the boat as it drifted towards the rocks. She'd been terrified it would smash against them and overturn. But luckily for her, it had continued to drift gently and finally had become wedged between the two biggest rocks.

'I know I called out then, Mum,' she whispered, her voice husky. 'I called and called and called, but no one heard.'

And then, as Christina's blue eyes clouded over, her mother's darker ones filled with tears and she took hold of her daughter's hand as she slipped back again into a semi-conscious state.

Chapter Eleven

For Christina's mother, the next forty-eight hours seemed an eternity as she sat beside her daughter's hospital bed, looking at her pale face, listening to her laboured breathing. For Áine, too, who in her short life had never seen anyone as ill as this, they were an eternity. And for Mr Doyle and Mrs Kenny, who prayed that Christina would make a full recovery, knowing that had she been able to confide in either of them this would never have happened. They now knew exactly what the problem had been. And to think that the bullying had been going on right under their noses!

Oh, they weren't fools, they were well aware that this type of thing went on at some time or other in most schools and that St Mary's was no exception, but the degree to which it had been allowed to develop unnoticed was most upsetting. Mr Doyle was determined that as soon as all this was over, he'd have a long talk with the whole school. Every pupil at St Mary's must be made aware of what to watch out for, must learn to observe the telltale signs in their classmates which might indicate they were being bullied and, most important of all, they had to be convinced that they must come forward and tell what was going on. Bullying at St Mary's would not be tolerated. In the meantime, he told himself, there was nothing else he or Mrs Kenny could do but wait anxiously for the phone call that would tell them the crisis was over.

And finally it was.

After two days and nights, the hospital doctor told Christina's mother that he felt the worst was over and that she should go back to the farm and get some rest. He was sure that when she came back, she would find her daughter fully awake and well enough to talk a little.

Áine was overjoyed when she heard the news and when Mr Doyle replaced the receiver of the telephone in his office, he let out a huge sigh of relief and offered up a silent prayer of thanks. Now, at last, he was ready to handle the pair who'd been the cause of all the trouble.

Bit by bit the whole unhappy story came out. Angela Miles couldn't believe all that her daughter had suffered at the hands of Siobhán and Helen, her two so-called friends. They'd played trick after cruel trick on her, tormenting her until she'd been driven almost to breaking-point. The lies they had told about her seeing another man and thinking of getting married again! It was hard to believe that two girls could be so vindictive, and for no reason that anyone could fathom. She only hoped that Mr Doyle would find a suitable punishment for both of them.

She still blamed herself for not noticing how troubled her daugher had been. 'I feel I've let you down badly, love. I was so taken up with my own problems that I didn't realise you had terrible problems of your own,' she said as she sat beside Christina in the hospital ward, the cold winter sunshine filtering in through a tall, narrow window.

'Don't worry about it, Mum. It's all over now, anyway.' Christina was sitting on an armchair and looking much better. 'How could you have known when I didn't give you a clue? I should have told you what was going on in the first place. It was foolish not to, I know that now, but at the time I thought I was doing the right thing.

'You were really frightened of them, weren't you?'

'Yes, oh yes,' her daughter answered softly.

Áine came to visit Christina every day after school, and the two friends were happy in each other's company. Sometimes Gráinne came too, and slowly Christina grew stronger.

The gloom which had hung over St Mary's had lifted as soon as word of Christina's recovery spread through the school. Everyone wondered what would happen next. After Mr Doyle's lecture the previous day the girls were in no doubt that the punishment would be severe. At best the two cuplrits would be suspended for several weeks, but if the headmaster so decided, they could be expelled. Rumour had it that when Siobhán and Helen were first questioned about their behaviour, they had vehemently denied everything, but when Patricia came forward and confessed that Siobhán had bullied her into lying to Christina about Mr Doyle wanting to see her, and then tricking her into doing all the extra homework, their innocent façade quickly began to crumble.

So far, no one knew what had taken place that day in Mr Doyle's office after the two girls had entered it, accompanied by their parents. Neither of them had appeared at their desks since, and no one knew when they'd be back.

'Gosh, that's great.' Christina smiled up at the doctor as he stood at the end of her bed. He'd just told her she could go home as soon as arrangements were made for someone to collect her.

Áine arrived in the ward as he was leaving, and looking after him asked, 'What'd he say that has you looking so happy?'

'I can go home, that's what,' said a delighted Christina.

'Brilliant, just brilliant. You'll come back to the farm, won't you, to recuperate for a while?' Áine asked excitedly

'Oh, I'd love to, but would Mum agree, do you think?'

'She already has,' Áine told her smugly. 'Mammy insisted on it. We've been doing some arranging while you were lying there in bed, miss, doing nothing but eating goodies and reading books.'

Christina laughed.

'Mammy knew your Mum was anxious about going back to work and leaving you alone in the house before you've fully recovered. So they had a chat about it, and it's OK with her, it's OK with my mother and....'

'It's definitely OK with me,' Christina finished for her, with a hearty laugh.

Chapter Twelve

Although the weather wasn't good enough for Christina to go out much, the two weeks she spent at the farm flew by. Áine's grandmother took her under her wing and she hardly had a chance to miss Áine and the twins while they were away at school. Just as Áine had said, her grandmother had an endless supply of tales to tell and within days Christina felt she'd known her all her life—and everyone else in Castledonagh, too. It was from Granny O'Neill that Christina learned that McDonagh's Ruin was reputed to be haunted.

'They say anyone who survives a night in that place will live to be a hundred,' she said. Christina didn't know whether or not she'd slept through any ghostly visitations on the night she spent there, but she had to laugh when the old woman had tapped her on the shoulder. 'So there you are now, child. You can look forward to drawing the old age pension for a very long time!'

Her mother rang every day to check her progress and Mr Doyle wrote her a long letter which put her mind completely at ease about how she'd be received when she returned to St Mary's. A huge 'Get Well' card arrived to which all her classmates had signed their names—all except two, that is!

The post never arrived at Woodville until mid-afternoon. Christina was surprised one day when Áine's mother called up to her from the kitchen, 'Letter for you, Christina.'

She hurried down from Áine's bedroom, where

she'd been sorting out her things in anticipation of her journey home in a few days' time. Christina studied the handwriting on the envelope, wondering who it could be from. It looked vaguely familiar, yet she couldn't be sure. Her eyes went immediately to the signature at the end of the second page. It read 'Helen.' Christina stared at the name, a strange cold feeling coming over her. It couldn't be starting again, could it? They couldn't be so cruel as to try to get at her even with all these miles between them. The blood drained from her face and the sheet of paper began to shake in her hand. Áine's mother hurried across the kitchen to where she stood and asked, 'What's the matter, Christina? Is there some bad news in your letter, love?'

'I...I haven't...read it yet,' she faltered. 'It's from...Helen.'

'From Helen? What on earth could she be writing to you about?' Áine's mother asked, as puzzled by the whole thing as Christina was. 'Well, go on then, read it.'

'I...can't,' Christina said as she passed the letter over to her. 'I'm afraid....they might be starting all over again,' she finished shakily.

'Now, don't worry. If it's anything like that, we'll put a stop to it immediately,' Maureen O'Neill said soothingly, as she began to scan what Helen had written.

'Well, who'd have thought that?' she said with a low whistle when she'd finished reading. She handed the letter back to Christina. 'Read away, love. There's nothing in it that will frighten you. As a matter of fact, you're in for quite a surprise.'

Dear Christina, the letter said

Please don't tear up this letter when you see it's from me. Just give me a chance to explain why I did such terrible things to you during the past couple of months. I know it's no excuse for my behaviour, but when I came to St Mary's last year I didn't know anyone. My family only moved into Glenwood just before Christmas and when I started school in January everyone in the class had already made friends.

As you know, Siobhán can be very charming when she wants to, and when she started paying special attention to me, I was really flattered. Whenever she passed smart remarks about people, I always agreed with her, although most of the time I didn't like it, but, above everything else, I didn't want to be an outsider. I just wanted a friend— even if it had to be Siobhán!

Remember the day we messed about with your pen? Well, because I agreed to go along with her, she had a hold over me after that and somehow I just couldn't break away. I think I was actually afraid of her. But when I realised she meant to go on and on tormenting you and never seemed to be satisfied that we'd done enough, I refused to help her trick you into doing all that extra homework. Then, of course, she began working on Patricia. I couldn't say anything to anyone then, either, Christina, as I'd already been her partner in so many terrible things.

But when you ran away, I really wanted to go to Mr Doyle and tell him what had been going on, especially when he spoke to us all that day at assembly. I told Siobhán what I intended to do and she got so mad that she actually hit me in the face. I was terrified of her after that and clammed up completely. I was afraid even to be seen

137

talking to anyone else in case she thought I was letting out on her. When Patricia eventually spoke out, I was so relieved. I knew then I could tell everything, that I wouldn't be alone any longer now that there were two of us.

Even though he didn't hold me fully to blame, Mr Doyle was really furious with me for not speaking up, so I've been suspended from school for a couple of weeks. But at least I'll be back soon. Siobhán won't be coming back at all.

She never really admitted why she decided to pick on you, but I think it had something to do with you and Áine being such good friends. She often told me how glad she was that Áine was gone. She knew she was always more popular than her, and that really made her mad, but she was afraid to try anything on Áine. I think she knew she wouldn't put up with it. As soon as Áine had left, in some strange way she saw you as a means of getting back at her.

Christina, if you're still reading this, please forgive me, I'm really, really sorry for everything. I know I've no right to think of it, but is there any chance that in the future we might even become friends?

Helen

Christina sat staring at the letter. She could hardly believe that all the time she was being teased and tormented by Siobhán, Helen was suffering too. It would never have occurred to her that Helen was being forced to act against her will. If only Helen had said something; between them maybe they'd have been able to stand up to Siobhán. But who was she to think that? Hadn't she made the same mistake as Helen by saying nothing and simply putting up with all Siobhán's terrible bullying. Poor Helen, she thought, then realised how strange it was that she should now be thinking sympathetically of Helen, when only minutes before, she had regarded her in the same light as Siobhán.

Glancing out the window, she saw the twins racing each other home after school. Áine followed at a more leisurely pace. Christina leaped off the bed, raced down the stairs and out to meet her. She couldn't wait to hear what Áine would have to say about Helen's letter.

'Jealous of me being popular!' Áine said, after reading Helen's letter. 'Can you believe it? She always had plenty of friends herself, as far as I could see.'

'Yes,' said Christina, 'she had friends all right. But when you think about it, she never seemed to stick with any of them for very long.'

'Maybe that was it,' agreed Áine.

'Unlike us, you mean?'

'Unlike us,' Áine confirmed, giving Christina an affectionate grin.

The car engine had been running for several minutes and still the girls hadn't appeared. Jim O'Neill blew the horn again and at last the two of them came strolling around the side of the house, dark and red heads close together.

'Mammy promised her sister we'd go up to Dublin to spend New Year's Eve with her,' Áine was telling her friend.

'That's terrific. We'll be able to meet up then. We

can organise a sleep-over at my house while you're in Dublin, and maybe we can go bowling at that new leisure complex I was telling you about. It's great knowing that we'll be seeing each other again in a month or so.'

'If not sooner!'

'What do you mean, Áine?'

'Oh, nothing,' Áine said vaguely, not managing to look as innocent as she'd have liked.

'Come on. I know you, you're planning something. Tell me what it is. Don't be so mean.'

'Patience, patience,' Áine said mysteriously.

Christina was not to be fobbed off so easily. 'What do you mean "patience"? I'm going in a few minutes. There isn't time to be patient!'

'Well, you see…' Áine began, but broke off as her father sounded the horn again.

'Come on, out with it. Your father's getting tired of waiting.'

Jim O'Neill folded his arms across his chest. 'I hate to rush you two ladies, but I *do* have an appointment, you know.'

It was then that Christina noticed that Áine's father was dressed in his best suit. Except for Mass on Sundays it was the first time she'd seen him out of working clothes since she'd been at the farm. She hadn't expected him to dress so formally just to drive her back to Dublin. As though reading her thoughts, Áine turned to Christina and said, 'I didn't want to tell you earlier. I wanted to save it until the last minute. You know, keep it as a surprise.'

Christina looked at her enquiringly.

'You see, there's just a chance we may be going

140

back home to Glenwood.'

'What?' Christina almost shouted.

'Yes. After Dad leaves you home today, he's got an interview with a subsidiary of his old company. They rang him the other day out of the blue, so we're all keeping our fingers crossed.'

Knowing he'd never split the girls up if he didn't do something drastic, Jim O'Neill took Christina by the shoulder and with an authoritative 'In,' pointed her in the direction of the open passenger door. Still speechless with surprise at what Áine had just said, Christina could only wave madly out the window at her friend, as the car began to bump its way down the boreen.

Bright Sparks

Saving the Dark Planet
by Mary Arrigan

Terrified fourteen-year-old **Aisling** finds herself and her little sister, **Cara**, in a claustrophobic spacecraft hurtling to an unknown galaxy. Cobi is a dark and barren place which has been destroyed by its own technology. The Cobians, desperate for survival, have abducted a group of people who will teach them the old skills. As the girls have little to offer will the cold-blooded Cobians use their bodies for cloning experiments? Will their organs be taken for transplant?

Saving the Dark Planet is an exciting adventure from the author of *Searching for the Green*.

Price: £4.99
ISBN: 1 85594 178 3

THE BRIGHT SPARKS FAN CLUB

WOULD YOU LIKE TO JOIN?

Would you like to receive a **FREE** bookmark and BRIGHT SPARKS friendship bracelet?

You are already halfway there. If you fill in the questionnaire on the opposite page and one other questionnaire from the back page of any of the other BRIGHT SPARKS titles and return both questionnaires to Attic Press at the address below, you automatically become a member of the BRIGHT SPARKS FAN CLUB.

If you are, like many others, a lover of the BRIGHT SPARKS fiction series and become a member of the BRIGHT SPARKS FAN CLUB, you will receive special discount offers on all new BRIGHT SPARKS books, plus a BRIGHT SPARKS bookmark and a beautiful friendship bracelet made with the BRIGHT SPARKS colours. Traditionally friendship bracelets are worn by friends until they fall off! If your friends would like to join the club, tell them to buy the books and become a member of this book lovers' club.

Please keep on reading and spread the word about our wonderful books. We look forward to hearing from you soon.

Name _____

Address _____

_____

Age _____

You can order your books by post, fax and phone direct from:
Attic Press, 29 Upper Mount St, Dublin 2, Ireland.
Tel: (01) 661 6128 Fax: (01) 661 6176

Attic Press hopes you enjoyed *Searching for a Friend*. To help us improve the **Bright Sparks** series for you please answer the following questions.

1. Why did you decide to buy this book?

_____

_____

_____

2. Did you enjoy this book? Why?

_____

_____

_____

3. Where did you buy it?

_____

_____

_____

4. What do you think of the cover?

_____

_____

_____

5. Have you ever read any other books in the **BRIGHT SPARKS** series? Which one/s?

_____

_____

_____

6. Have you any comments to make on the books in the **BRIGHT SPARKS** series?

_____

_____

_____

If there is not enough space for your answers on this coupon please continue on a sheet of paper and attach it to the coupon.

Post this coupon to **Attic Press**, 29 Upper Mount Street, Dublin 2 and we'll send you a **BRIGHT SPARKS** bookmark.

Name_____Age_____
Address _____
_____Date_____

You can order your books by post, fax and phone direct from:
Attic Press, 29 Upper Mount St, Dublin 2. Ireland.
Tel: (01) 661 6128 Fax: (01) 661 6176